The Tao of Mermaids

Unlocking the Universal Code with the Angels and Mermaids

Kitty Bishop, Ph.D.

BALBOA.
PRESS

Balboa Press books may be ordered through booksellers or by contacting:

Balboa Press
A Division of Hay House
1663 Liberty Drive
Bloomington, IN 47403
www.balboapress.com
1-(877) 407-4847

Because of the dynamic nature of the Internet, any Web addresses or links contained in this book may have changed since publication and may no longer be valid. The views expressed in this work are solely those of the author and do not necessarily reflect the views of the publisher, and the publisher hereby disclaims any responsibility for them.

The author of this book does not dispense medical advice or prescribe the use of any technique as a form of treatment for physical, emotional, or medical problems without the advice of a physician, either directly or indirectly. The intent of the author is only to offer information of a general nature to help you in your quest for emotional and spiritual well-being. In the event you use any of the information in this book for yourself, which is your constitutional right, the author and the publisher assume no responsibility for your actions.

Any people depicted in stock imagery provided by Thinkstock are models, and such images are being used for illustrative purposes only.
Certain stock imagery © Thinkstock.

ISBN: 978-1-4525-0064-5 (sc)
ISBN: 978-1-4525-0063-8 (e)

Library of Congress Control Number: 2010914835

Printed in the United States of America

Balboa Press rev. date: 11/5/2010

Dedication

To those who have not forgotten how to dream and still believe in
six impossible things before breakfast.
Shine on, you crazy diamond!

*Those who dream by day are cognizant of many things which escape
those who dream only by night.*

Edgar Allan Poe (1809 - 1849)

Contents

Chapter 1

The Elixir of Life

I sat upon a promontory
And heard a mermaid, on a dolphin's back,
Uttering such dulcet and harmonious breath
That the rude sea grew civil at her song,
And certain stars shot madly from their spheres
To hear the sea-maid's music.
- William Shakespeare (A Midsummer Night's Dream)

Water Magic

I have always felt drawn to mermaids. My husband Charles, who is a musician, even named his recording studio *Mermaid Studios* because we always joked that I was a mermaid accidentally born on land. I was born under the astrological constellation of Pisces, a water sign. Pisces is the sign of the planet Venus, the Roman goddess of love. The planet Venus found its highest spiritual expression during the age of Pisces, which is now nearing its final years. Venus is the renamed Greek goddess Aphrodite, who was sea born and has a very special and profound connection with the Ocean. Her sacred animal is the dolphin.

With my long, naturally blonde and wavy hair I even look like a mermaid. I love water and spend as much time as I can near it, especially oceans. When I was younger, I was a rescue swimmer and I was given my gold level medal in swimming (which involved rescuing a drowning person, diving and retrieving objects and

1

swimming underwater for the full length of the pool) in the summer when I was 15. I am magnetically attracted by animals that represent the water element, such as dolphins, sea turtles and sea horses.

I have a strong research interest in Lemuria and Atlantis, the "lost" and submerged continents, paired with a powerful feeling that I have access to the information of these civilizations and seeing scenes and images from those days vividly in full color and in clear detail in front of me when I read something that sparks a memory, or ignites my imagination.

My diet naturally gravitates towards salty foods, sea vegetables, sea food and Asian cooking which is light and sea-based. Water tastes sweet and wonderful to me. It really feels life-giving on a soul level. I drink at least 8 glasses of water a day. Running water is music to my ears and my house and garden do not feel complete without a water fountain, a pond or a wishing well in it.

Unsurprisingly, once I followed my own inner guidance, I gave birth easily and painlessly to my second son, Elias—a Rainbow child—at home in water, laughing throughout the birth which took place during a dark, cozy, welcoming winter night.

I was still writing my book about the magic of the unicorns and the message they have for humankind that divine love really is the key to manifesting everything we desire, including our life purpose, when the mermaids started to enter my meditations. Professionally, I work with healing crystals and jewelry and, as I have always loved pearls and wear them daily, I feel very close to the vibration and energy they emit.

Pearl, I was told, is in fact one of the five unicorn jewels, which means that the vibration of pearls harmonizes with the energy of the unicorns and amplifies it.

As I started to work with pearls in my meditations and dreams, the Mermaids, who love pearls and feel a kinship with them, used this connection to communicate a vivid image to me. I saw myself clearly as a Mermaid, floating and diving in the water towards the sea floor below me. At first, I was in wild abandon, purely enjoying my freedom, immersed in the warm water all around me, but gradually I became aware of a blurred shape at the bottom of the sea.

As I drew closer, the picture became clearer and I could see that I was swimming towards an old, wooden treasure chest with a lid held open by metal hinges, which was sparkling with the light of uncountable gold coins. The warm glow emitting from the wooden treasure chest beamed into the unfathomable depth of the sea around it.

Gazing at the limitless and effortless abundance before me, I had a sense of welcome, of joy, of infinite possibility and potential. I was impressed with a feeling of significance. At one level, the Mermaids were simply showing me the age-old image of the Mermaid's treasure, which represents their abundance and manifestation skills, but I felt that the deeper, or hidden, message in this vision was the joyful abandon with which mermaids embrace the water element and the principle of the *Tao*.

I knew when I had this vision that my next book was going to be about the Mermaids and the magic of the water element, but beyond that I had no idea of the content. I intended to call this book *Mermaid Magic* or *Mermaid Messages* but I felt that an important element was missing from these titles. One day, as I was improvising and playing around with the title page, I suddenly found myself typing *The Tao of Mermaids*. Although I had studied the Taoist teachings intensively, I had never considered this title, or the connection between mermaids and the *Tao*, before.

What is the Tao?

The term *tao* or *dao* can alternatively be read as *dào*, meaning "way" or *dǎo*, meaning "guide". The concept of *Tao* is found in Taoism, Confucianism, and more generally in ancient Chinese philosophy. Tao both precedes and encompasses the universe; it is a signifier for the One, the All, the First Cause or Source.

If you want to picture an origin—a beginning—imagine this: In the beginning there was an ocean of Spirit (the Tao) which filled all of space. Every particle was alive, intelligent and vibrating. The Spirit was static, content, and aware of itself. It was formless Beingness, resting on the bosom of its thought and contemplating That Which It Is.

Then the moment came when Spirit moved into action. It contracted into itself until all of space was a void at the centre of which the inquiring mind of the Spirit shone as a dazzling white light which illuminated itself. This activity marked the advent of the individuality of the Spirit.

The Spirit—the Tao—discovered itself anew in all the manifestations it could take. In this way, the Spirit could experience itself through its outflowings, or extensions, or conduits—a myriad of infinite souls. The Spirit is always growing, always expanding. Experience is how it learns. This Spirit was the Tao; the Divine Matrix, Alpha and Omega, All That Is, the One, the All, or God.

Why did the Infinite seek to individualize itself? It desired self-expression and desired companionship; therefore, it projected the cosmos and individual souls, who are divine sparks flying from the divine flame of light. The cosmos was built with music, arithmetic, geometry, harmony, system, and balance.

The cosmic building blocks were all of the same material—Tao, or the life essence.

It was this Divine Power that changed the length of its wave and the rate of its vibration which created the blueprint for multitudes of forms. This action resulted in the law of diversity which allowed for an infinite number of patterns. Tao, or Source, used the law of diversity like a pianist plays the piano—creating melodies and arranging them into a symphony.

Each design carries within it the plan for its evolution. This plan corresponds to a single note played on the piano. The sounds of several notes unite to make a chord; chords in turn become phrases; phrases become melodies; melodies interact and dance with each other; moving back and forth, across and between and around each other, to make a symphony. Then in the end, there comes a final note and the music stops playing because the arrangement is complete. At this point, the physical universe will be no more; but in the space between the first note and the finale there was wondrous beauty, splendid creativity and magnificent experience. Tao, or Spirit, always *is*, without beginning or end. The Spiritual universe will continue, and all souls will continue to expand and evolve from the vantage point of divine expression.

All manifest things are a part of Tao (the One, God) and an expression of Tao. The Universal Mind of God was the force which propelled and perpetuated these thoughts. All minds are conduits of Source energy and express the thoughts of God. Hence, everything we do, feel, or think is in the Mind of Tao. We do what Tao imagines, or thinks. Because we are eternally part of the One, we are privy to all the powers of the One. The universe is always on our side. Everything that came into being is an aspect of the One Mind.

As the Austrian mystic and educator Rudolf Steiner (1861 – 1925) writes: "In the spiritual world all is in perpetual mobile activity in the process of ceaseless creating. A state of rest ... does not exist here because the archetypes [blueprints] are creative beings. They are the master builders of all that comes into being in the physical and soul worlds." [1]

The *Tao Te Ching*, a famous philosophical tract which has been attributed to Laozi (also transcribed as Lao Tse or Lao Tzu) who lived from 600 BC - 531 BC, describes the material world of creation as "the named" or "the ten thousand things". Material reality is seen as consisting of physical manifestations of Tao and, as such, it can only operate within the principle and laws of Tao. Tao is often referred to as "the nameless" because neither it nor its principles can ever be adequately expressed in words.

However, while the Tao cannot be expressed, it *can* be known, and its principles *can* be followed. This is often expressed in *yin* and *yang* polarity, where every action creates a counter-action as a natural, unavoidable movement within manifestations of the Tao. We can visualize this principle of the Tao as like a boomerang, which returns to us exactly what we send out.

Karma is another word for this principle. *Karma* is a Sanskrit word, meaning "action". It is a neutral and objective term which does not refer to punishment, guilt or shame but rather is a universal law which is precise, infallible and responsive to our every thought, word and action. In this way, the principle is unmovable, fair and generous

Understanding this principle leads to selflessness, faith
and divine love. We realize that we are a child of Tao (or
the Divine Matrix; God). This can be compared with
the Buddhist notion of *anatta* (no-self) which recognizes
that we do not have a self, or an ego, separate from the
Void (the Nameless, the One, the All).

In Taoism, Tao is understood in terms of three constituents, just
as God is understood as a threefold divinity in Christianity. *Jing*
corresponds to energy (Father); *Qi* refers to the flow of energy (Son);
and *Shen* is the Spirit (Holy Spirit). Of course, Tao or God is not
literally split into three parts; the threefold divinity merely describes
different aspects of the One Source; the One Substance.

Thus, the trinity *Jing Qi Shen* constitutes the Tao of All That Is.
They are represented as deities in the Three Pure Ones.

"Manna" or the Elixir of Life

Mermaids represent the spirit of the water element. Our bodies
are 70% water and if we do not replenish this water regularly, our
body can no longer function. Drinking pure, clean water is one of
the most important acts we can perform to keep our bodies and
minds running smoothly. Metaphysically, "drinking" can be seen as
a symbolic action representing internalizing or becoming.

In mysticism, the Elixir of Life, which is also known as the
Elixir of Immortality and sometimes equated with the Philosopher's
Stone of the alchemists and the *manna* of the ancient Hebrews, is
a legendary potion that grants eternal life, or eternal youth to the
person partaking of it. Many practitioners of alchemy thought of
the potion as real and searched for the recipe that would allow them
to reconstitute the drink and give them access to its powers. The
Elixir of Life was said to be so powerful, that not only could it grant
eternal life to its drinker, but beyond that it even had the power to
create life itself.

When you partake of *manna*, the gifts bestowed on you are said
to include telepathy, levitation, and the ability to walk on water.
It is said that *manna* (which the Greek termed *ambrosia* or the

nectar of the Gods) takes the drinker beyond the ordinary human four dimensional space-time continuum and transforms him or her into a fifth dimensional being surrounded by brilliant white light; unbound by material laws, and possessing supreme healing and miracle powers.

In Revelations (2:17 KJV) we read the following: "He that hath an ear, let him hear what the Spirit saith unto the churches; To him that overcometh will I give to eat of the hidden *manna*, and will give him a white stone, and in the stone a new name written, which no man knoweth saving he that receiveth it." This bible passage holds the key to a less literal interpretation of the legendary elixir that bestows immortality on anybody who drinks it.

The Angel Symbol of the Hidden Manna

The act of drinking a potion or eating hidden (secret) *manna* can be interpreted to symbolize the act of internalizing, integrating and *becoming*. The "white stone" or "hidden manna" referred to in the Bible is given to those who overcome illusion, erroneous belief and unlawful thinking—which are always based on a mistaken awareness of our true nature, or authentic self, and a separation from God.

The "new name" that we receive when we have healed our separation from God is the name (nature) of our authentic Self, which "no man knoweth" because it is an internal experience. The Elixir of Life is really a non-physical and cognizant realization of the soul's true origin, meaning and purpose.

In truth, there is no death. The body may disintegrate in divine timing; but our true self, our soul, is immortal and one with God, as an individualized expression of Divine consciousness. Jesus understood the immortality of each individual soul when he said: "He is not the God of the dead, but the God of the living; for all live unto Him." (Luke 20:38 KJV)

Enoch, Thoth, Hermes and Archangel Metatron

This "magic potion" is like a red thread which weaves through the life stories of the prophet Enoch, Thoth (the Egyptian God of the Moon, Magic and Writing) and Hermes Trismegistus, all of whom are reported to have consumed "the white drops" or the "white powder of gold" as the elixir was also called—thereby achieving immortality.

Fascinatingly, these distinct and significant personalities are in actuality one soul, or one stream of consciousness, in successive incarnations; assuming different names and physical forms.

Enoch was a prophet who is thought to have lived in the third century B.C. According to the biblical narrative (Genesis 5:21-24), Enoch lived 365 years, which is a far shorter life span than that of the other patriarchs in the period before the Flood. Enoch was the first to invent books and writing, much like Thoth the scribe. The ancient Greeks confirm that Enoch is the same soul entity as Mercury and Hermes Trismegistus, who wrote the *Emerald Tablets of Thoth*.

Enoch discovered the knowledge of the Zodiac, and the course of the Planets; and he emphasized to his followers that the worship of God was the highest good. The prophet Enoch and his disciples left Babylon for Egypt. There he continued his mission, reminding people of the principles of justice and fairness, teaching selected prayers and instructing on the benefits of fasting on certain days and generosity of spirit, which included the practical act of charity— giving a portion of one's income to the disadvantaged and poor and thus, ideally, helping them to help themselves.

In the Hebrew language, Enoch's name stood for "Initiate" or "Initiator". The *Book of Enoch* in its original Aramaic version was lost until several Dead Sea Scroll fragments were discovered in Qumran, providing parts of the Aramaic original. One of these original fragments reads: "Humankind is called on to observe how unchanging nature follows God's will." [2]

At the end of his life, Enoch "walked with God", who turned him into the Archangel Metatron.

Thoth was considered one of the principal deities of the Egyptian pantheon, often depicted with the head of an Ibis. His feminine counterpart is Seshat. His chief shrine was at Khemennu (where he led the pantheon), later renamed Hermopolis by the Greeks, in reference to Thoth, because the Greeks were aware that he was the same entity as Hermes.

The writings of Enoch and Thoth on the "sacred knowledge of creation" are remarkably similar. One of Thoth's honorary titles, "three times great", was translated into Greek as Trismegistos, thereby giving us Hermes Trismegistus.

In several of his past-life readings, the famous American psychic Edgar Cayce (1877 – 1945) informs us that Hermes or Thoth was an engineer from the submerging Atlantis and that he either built, or designed, or oversaw the construction of the Pyramids of Egypt.

The Angels on "Amrita", the Nectar of Life

In the Hindu scriptures, we find the parallel imagery of *Amrita*, or the Elixir of Life. It is written that anybody who consumes just a drop of *Amrita* gains immortality. The legend recounts that in early times when the inception of the world had just taken place, evil demons gained strength. The gods saw this as a threat because they had a deep-seated fear of evil.

The gods Indra, the god of rain; Vayu, the god of wind; and Agni, the god of fire, went to seek advice and help from the Creator—represented in three aspects according to the Vedic tradition as Vishnu, the preserver; Brahma, the creator; and Shiva, the destroyer.

Vishnu, Brahma, and Shiva suggested that *Amrita* could only be gained from the action of *samudra manthan* (churning of the ocean) for the ocean hid mysterious and secret objects in its unfathomable depths.

Vishnu agreed to take the form of a turtle on whose shell a huge mountain was placed. With the help of a mighty and long serpent the churning process began at the surface of the ocean. The snake had curled itself around the mountain. The gods pulled the serpent from one side while the demons pulled it from the other side.

The churning process required immense strength. The demons were persuaded to do the work in return for a portion of *Amrit*. Finally, with the combined effort of the gods and demons, *Amrit* emerged from the depths of the ocean. The gods were offered the drink but they succeeded in tricking the demons who did not partake of the sacred potion.

I asked the Angels for a metaphysical interpretation of this story. They explained to me that the "evil demons" referred to in this story symbolize the shadow side of our being, the personality or ego part of us that is made up of pain, fear, guilt, resentment, shame, hatred, judgment and other negative, destructive and ill-making emotions. These aspects of ourselves are created by a willful turning away from truth, honesty, openness, joy and gratitude. Happiness is our natural state. In the absence of any thought, when we don't think at all, we are perfectly happy.

It is only when we start to think in ways that negate our True Nature, which is always connected, always joyful, and always *alive*, that we feel negative ("evil") emotions. In the same way, demons are negative thought forms that can appear real and have a real influence on us if we allow them in. Negative emotions and "evil demons" appear and feel real to us and we buy into the illusion when we give them our energy and attention; that is, our power.

All healing ritual, whether it is rosewater, incense, medicine, prayer and so forth, essentially has only one aim—to assist us in aligning our vibrations with who we truly are; our real self. All healing ultimately comes from the Self, and there is no exception to that.

Humans have been granted Free Will—which includes the choice to turn away from their true nature—in an experiment by the Creative Forces who desire to experience themselves through us and in us, in all aspects, while remaining ever with us and ensuring that in the end (remember, time as we know it does not exist outside the human experience) we all return "home"; in other words, we live in perfect harmony and expression of the Law.

The Angels and Ascended Masters are an articulation of this self-realized consciousness and show us what the human soul really is. The potential of the human soul is omnipresent, or ever-there. It is built into your matrix; your design.

Mermaid Exercise: How to Read Your Emotions

You can always know exactly how connected you are to your Soul (your Higher Self, or Inner Being), and how much of your true self you are expressing, by the way you feel.

The Mermaids, who rule the water element and the emotional side of our nature, suggest that you stop what you are doing for a split second, take a deep breath and ask yourself: "How do I feel *right now*? Do I feel less than good; maybe angry, or resentful, or judgmental, or dismissive, or hurt, or vengeful, or depressed?"

The Mermaids say that if the answer is "yes" (and be honest with this!), what you are manifesting when you have these feelings is, momentarily, not in agreement with the perspective of your Soul, or authentic self. This broader perspective part of you is always one with the Creator, and knows that you truly are eternally joyful, happy, blessed, loving and peaceful.

The Mermaids say that when we are in harmony with our true self, expressing who we are at the soul level and living our life's purpose, we feel wonderful. When we feel the sheer pleasure, joy and exhilaration of being *alive*, uplifting and inspiring those around us by just *being ourselves*, we know that we are "on track", manifesting and living exactly the life our Soul planned for us prior to coming into this body, on this planet, at this time.

The Mermaids have a very important job to do. They are here to assist us with moving our feelings and emotions—the domain of the water element—up the pole towards its highest, best feeling point, which is simultaneously the fullest expression of our soul's purpose. To accomplish this, the Mermaids work with the magic of the water element and join forces with the Angels, Ascended Masters and Spirit Guides (especially dolphins) as well as with Crystals, Colors and Light Ray Energy to heal our heart chakra, manifest our light body, and prepare us for the next step in evolution.

our beliefs and wounds regarding sexuality, the physical body and our emotions. They also incorporate the healing qualities of water and can assist us in cleansing physically, emotionally, mentally and spiritually. The Merfolk exist all over the world in the oceans and seas. The Mermaids and Mermen of Atlantis, however, are considered to be the "royalty" of the Merpeople. These Merpeople are some of the great protectors, alongside the Angels of Atlantis, of the healing crystals and temples of Atlantis, which are now submerged under sea water and lie in the depths of the Ocean.

Mer-Angels

There are also other Mermaids and Mermen who help to protect the oceans and seas, and the healing crystals and temples of Atlantis. There are mermaids who are known as "Mer-Angels" and some who are known as "Mer-Fairies". The Mer-Angels are Mermaids and Mermen who are like the Archangels of the Oceans. They have a fish tail, like regular mermaids, paired with large angel wings extending from the back of their human torso. The Mer-Fairies are smaller Mermaids and Mermen with fish tails and gossamer wings like that of a filigree-winged fairy.

During a workshop I attended a couple of years ago, in 2008, we were instructed to close our eyes and feel our wings. While everybody else sensed insect-like filigree wings reminiscent of a butterfly or a dragonfly, I felt something soft, smooth and feathery between my shoulder blades. Although I feel strongly that I combine the missions of the angels and the mermaids in this incarnation, I have not shared this inner knowledge with anyone except my husband Charles. Recently, I received the following letter from Nathalie, a very intuitive friend of mine:

> *I didn't get to tell you fully at the time but when we were sitting together in the chalice gardens [The Chalice Well Gardens in Glastonbury, England] and I saw green and orange around your head, it was quite a profound experience for me. I know this means healing and creativity for you and I admire hugely what you have achieved with your health and life purpose. I*

also found you literally glowing with beauty when I looked directly at you and I am sure you are a merangel as I think you already know.

The Mer-Angels and Mer-Fairies often work very closely with the Incarnated Merpeople to ensure the wellbeing of the Oceans and aquatic life. An Incarnated Mermaid is a soul who was a Mermaid in a past life and who made the decision to incarnate in a human body in this life in order to help educate humanity on how to treat the Oceans and the Earth in beneficial and healthy ways. Mer-Angels combine the body of a mermaid, complete with fish tail and long wavy hair, with the white feathery wings of an angel. On a soul level, they combine qualities of both.

I believe that my soul is like an angel that dwells in the mermaid realms. In addition to embodying many mermaid characteristics, I also identify with many of the attributes of incarnated angels.

My personality is calm, peaceful and loving. My metabolism actively responds to sugar and I have cut it out of my diet completely because I suffer draining health and energy effects from it. After just two weeks of eating no sugar at all, everything started to taste very sweet to me and I now find the taste of pure sugar, or sugary foods, too (sickly) sweet for my taste buds.

My lips are full, expressive and bowed. My hair is naturally blond, wavy and soft. One of the most frequent comments I get from people is that I seem to glow. I can be sociable and love to communicate (the moon in my birth chart is in Gemini) but I also enjoy my quiet alone time reading and meditating and prefer to work with people one-on-one or in small groups.

I have a Ph.D. in transpersonal counseling and often find myself occupying a counseling role in my relationships. I am a perfectionist who enjoys breaking the rules when I see a better way of doing things. When I follow my heart, the outcome always exceeds my expectations. I do not like to get too close to many people. I have a small circle of trusted family members and friends whom I hold very close to my heart and I feel protective of my personal boundaries.

My appetite fluctuates with my moods. I am very empathic and my body senses other people's feelings. I have a tendency to give too much away to others because I see the good, and the soul's potential, in others before I see their negative traits. I developed medulloblastoma, a malignant brain tumor in 2006 and 2010. I underwent a series of operations and treatments until I gained the insight that I had to heal myself on all levels—physical, emotional, mental and spiritual—in order to cure myself completely and release the cancer permanently from my being.

Louise Hay's book *You Can Heal Your Life* affirmed to me that cancer is an illness, a *dis-ease* of resentment that is held onto for a long time, until it is externalized and the body literally starts to eat itself. My last operation was in March 2010 and, as I have had the maximum dosage of radiotherapy, and chemotherapy is not effective for my specific type of brain cancer, the medical profession and I agree that I have to keep myself alive and well by non-medical means, which (for me) involves nutrition, ayurvedic herbal tablets and the practice of Yoga and meditation.

I know that I have evolved from mermaid consciousness to the angelic consciousness because the spiritual lessons that I work on repeatedly in this life are the lessons of an angelic soul, or a soul on the ascension pathway, returning to God. I have learned how to overcome co-dependent relationships, how to look after myself and how to create emotional and etheric boundaries with others. I can now say "no" in situations where this is required.

I have learned how to speak up for myself, and to voice my own truth even if it is at odds with what others around me are saying, doing or believing. Incidentally, when I learned this lesson, my constant throat problems which showed themselves as recurring bronchitis, tonsillitis, sore throats, fever and loss of voice disappeared completely. I share the story of this healing in depth in my book *Unicorn Magic*.

My relationships with people are supportive, inspiring and uplifting. I have a strong desire to help people with the gifts, skills and talents I have been given in this incarnation.

ARE MERMAIDS REAL?

Elemental and angelic realms are real, as real as you and me. Mermaids are magical spiritual helpers who exist on the etheric plane and who are prepared to assist us. The etheric realms are invisible to human eyes because they are at a different vibration to the wave bands accessed by human sight (like radio waves or infrared light) but they can be seen with the third eye, or felt with the psychic senses. They are also logically deductible from Hermetics ("everything vibrates") and scientifically inferable from quantum physics. We either originate from these realms or take soul "breaks" in them after a difficult life on earth. People who come from the same realm, or souls who have spent time in the same kingdom, associating with similar souls, share common experiences.

I have vivid memories of complaining to my parents as a child about the size of sea horses. I just knew that some sea horses were in actuality very large and not small like the specimens we find in the sea today. Just like regression therapy work and autosuggestion or (self-)hypnosis, journeying into elemental and angelic realms is healing because these realms are filled with light.

Of course, you do not need to identify exclusively with one particular realm or feel that you are a specific type of incarnated earth angel. Many lightworkers, healers and evolved souls have spent passages of their soul journey in more than one realm. You might identify with the description of an incarnated mermaid or incarnated angel but are concerned that you might not "fit the image" because you bear no outer resemblance to one.

It might help you to see it like this: All of our souls are evolving in the heart and soul of an angel. Or, as Michelangelo, the angelic artist, said: "I saw the angel in the marble and carved until I set him free." In other words, we are all learning and moving towards re-unification with Source, or God. The angels have completed the soul journey and show us a shining example of what the soul truly is.

The angels are living embodiments of human potential and they show us what the elevation of mass consciousness into the fifth dimension—where we live from unconditional love—is all about.

You can never judge another, or yourself. A person who looks like an angel may be a younger earth soul just entering here after a sojourn in the angelic realms or they may be on a mission of service and identify with angelic qualities. Even if you do not outwardly fit the image we hold of an angel, if you identify with angelic qualities, it is likely that your soul has spent time in the angelic realms and was instructed and taught by souls there, or you may have developed angelic consciousness while living on earth.

The Mermaids can work with any of us no matter where we live. In the physical world, the third dimension, I am writing this in the fertile green mystical Vale of Avalon in Glastonbury, England. But our consciousness is connected with the consciousness of all, and therefore we are capable of travelling to various realms and locations if we desire to do so, without using our physical bodies.

We frequently go on magnificent and eventful voyages to other realms during our dream state, but, although all the information gets stored in our subconscious, in our conscious state we are usually unaware of this.

When we are meditating and visualizing scenes like swimming with the Mermaids of Atlantis, a part of our consciousness really does go to the depths of the Ocean where Atlantis and the Mermaids of Atlantis reside. We can experience remarkable healings and astonishing insights when we "travel" in this way.

Exercise: Healing with the Mermaids and Mermen of Atlantis

Sit or lie down in a comfortable position. Close your eyes and allow your entire body to completely relax. Take three deep breaths and surround yourself with a cocoon of sparkling white light, which divinely protects you. Call upon Archangel Michael, or another angel close to your heart, to be with you, hold you in his light and let only loving energies come through.

See yourself standing on a peaceful, exquisite beach. Above you is the azure blue sky, you can feel the shimmering white sand between your toes, and you are gazing serenely at the turquoise ocean in front of you. You sense the big, sturdy ferns and lush tropical vegetation around you while the wind gently plays with your hair and the sun warms you gently with a golden brilliance.

You can now see your Guardian Angel approach you from a distance. His or her wings sparkle in the sunlight, magnificent and protective, glowing in a rainbow of mesmerizing colors. His or her body emanates pure white light.

Your angel reaches you and gestures towards the ocean, saying: "The Mermaids and Mermen of Atlantis wish to purify you of old karmic patterns and negativity which no longer serve you. All negative energy within your aura, body and mind will be cleansed and transmuted. Divine Love and self-acceptance will replace any guilt, shame and resentment. When you are thus cleansed, they will infuse you with the powerful healing energies of the Crystals of Atlantis."

Feeling the soft sand beneath your feet, you walk towards the ocean until you feel the calm water embracing your ankles. As you go further and submerge yourself under the water you know that you continue to be able to breathe with ease, deeply and normally. As you float and paddle around, enjoying your freedom in the water, you make out three beautiful Mermaids and three handsome Mermen playing in the water.

They indicate for you to follow them further down into the depths of the Ocean to the healing temples and crystals of Atlantis. You swim easily and as the warm water envelopes you, you begin to feel lighter, relaxed and peaceful.

Now you approach a magnificent, glittering and sparkling temple with high pillars and adorned with symbolic ornaments. The temple radiates a rainbow of colors which seem to stroke you and heal your heart with their purity and brilliance.

You make out a large doorway leading to the temple's entrance, which is guarded by two magnificent Mer-Angels, one female and one male. As you approach the temple, you see many kinds of crystals resting on the ocean floor.

Their colors are vibrant, radiant and beautiful. You see pink rose quartz, clear quartz, violet amethyst, yellow citrine, green the name we use for the stone today. The brilliant blue crystal soon became popular with locals and tourists, and its origins were traced to the extinct volcanoes in the mountains of Barahona, where mining subsequently began.

This magnificent mineral may have remained a secret had it not been for the disseminated crystals which travelled along the streams and rivers, finding their way to the ocean. The Angels have told me that Larimar is a gift to humans from Mother Nature who made sure it was brought to daylight from its hidden crevices deep in the Earth to be "discovered" along the beach. There are many messages locked inside this crystal and humans have yet to understand and access all of them.

Because of its origin, Larimar is a delicate stone. When you have found one that speaks to you and that you wish to work with, always ensure that you store the crystal away from direct sunlight. Larimar can and will fade, even in incandescent lighting, and excess temperatures can adversely affect the stone's etheric frequencies as well.

Larimar crystals, like the Mermaids, love water. The blue crystal waits submerged underwater in Dominican mines until it is brought out in the open and exposed to bright light.

Larimar has the power to help soul mates to find one another while healing and transforming repetitive, unresolved patterns and negative karma between soul mates and lovers.

Larimar is finely tuned to the human body, especially the throat chakra. This area is associated with expression and inter-human communication and relationships. This chakra contains the thymus gland, which regulates the immune system, and the thyroid and parathyroid glands (near the trachea, or wind pipe), which secrete hormones to regulate growth and metabolism.

Larimar is known to stimulate the heart, throat, third eye and crown chakras, facilitating inner wisdom, authentic communication and outer manifestation. This crystal radiates peace, calm and serenity and can assist you with connecting with your personal independence and the well of creative energy inside you.

The blue color of Larimar reflects Divine consciousness, which grants freedom from self-imposed limitations and a sense of peace when the true self is finally accepted and embraced. The many beneficial properties of Larimar are based on a profound acceptance of the self.

When you accept and love yourself, everything else—prosperity, love, soul mate relationships, friendship, success, joy, security and peace—follows naturally. This self-acceptance, which is accompanied by an opening and an activation of the heart chakra, is the Mermaid's mission, and their message and frequency is solidified and materialized in the Larimar crystal.

As a crystal energy intuitive, I find that this stone is amazingly tuned into the energies of the human body, making it an outstanding healing tool. The following is a list of Larimar's many beneficial properties that I use in my consultation with clients and in my crystal healing practice.

- Calming; decreases stress, anxiety and guilt
- Brings peace, serenity, and tranquility
- Unites mind and thoughts with the heart and emotions
- Facilitates an open, receptive mind when confronted with change
- Stone of answers and truths
- Aids communication—also with dolphins and sea creatures
- Represents and supports peace, clarity, healing, and love
- Protects against negative energy
- Heals on all levels: physical, emotional, mental, spiritual
- Physically, particularly beneficial for the thymus, thyroid, and immune system

island off the coast of southeast Africa, and Myanmar (Burma). Interestingly, these places are islands (Sri Lanka and Madagascar) or have an ocean shore (Myanmar).

In Vedic astrology, the Blue Sapphire is known as *Neelam* or *Sauri Natna*, which translates to Saturn's stone, or *Shani Priya*, which means beloved of Saturn.

Kashmir (a province in Northern India) produced Sapphires which are legendary today. Kashmir Sapphires were found in a very remote mountainous region of India in the late 19th century. The stones were exceptionally pure in quality. The term "cornflower blue" for the particular brilliant blue color of the stone was coined from Kashmir sapphires. The color hue of the stone is often described as "velvety" or "sleepy" because it is extraordinarily appealing, calming and peaceful. The Sapphire deposit in Kashmir was exhausted by the 1920s and there have been no new finds in the region since.

There is an ancient Persian myth which paints a picture of a giant Blue Sapphire that Mother Earth rests upon. According to the legend, the sky is the reflection of this titan blue crystal.

Blue Sapphire focuses intent and awareness. It brings joy, prosperity and inner peace. Blue Sapphire is a widely used healing stone; an opener of the third eye. It is a spiritual gemstone that inspires spirituality and spiritual expression. This blue gemstone connects the higher mind with the spiritual centers of the human body, and is a cleanser and purifier. Blue Sapphire emits a powerful and transformative energy. It facilitates self-expression, assisting in communication and expressing your truth and beliefs.

Like other blue Mermaid crystals, it purifies and heals the Throat Chakra and the associated thyroid gland and has a calming and balancing effect on the brain and nervous system. Blue Sapphire helps you to stay on the spiritual path, releasing blockages and providing strength. It opens the Third Eye and helps manifest one's life purpose and karmic agreements for soul growth.

Pink Sapphire resonates with the Heart Chakra and clears emotional blockages, bringing peace and unconditional love.

Mermaid Colors

The Mermaids' mission is to heal the Heart Chakra and to help us be whole and healthy on a physical level so that we may manifest love in a spiritual, divine way. To this end, they work with the water element and the color frequency blue, but they also resonate with pink, which is the color of the heart and love.

Pink Sapphires have recently become widely available because new deposits were found in Madagascar in the late 1990s. Until this time, pure Pink Sapphires were exceptionally rare and were found only in a few locations in Vietnam, Sri Lanka and Myanmar. The recent discovery of Pink Sapphire, which vibrates to the frequency of the Heart Chakra, in superior quality and quantity in southern Madagascar has caused the demand for this gemstone to increase greatly.

Angel Message on Pink Sapphires

On a spiritual level, the Angels have told me that this find of Pink Sapphires has come about because more people are tuning in the Heart Energy and the Heart Chakra, healing and activating it. If you are drawn to pure white, vibrant green or pink colors and crystals, you are actively engaged in work that involves the Heart Chakra and you are called to purify and open it. Madagascar Pink Sapphire displays a full range of color hues from a very pale delicate pink to a vivid, almost magenta, intense cerise tone.

Numerology: 1 (Blue Sapphire)
Zodiac: Gemini. Associated with Saturn. Portal to Heavenly Realms and Angelic Messages.
Birth Stone: September
Chakra: Throat (Blue Sapphire); Heart (Pink and Green Sapphires)
Element: Water
Planet: Moon

Moonstone can have a strong cooling effect and in some individuals this may lead to a disbalance in the energy system leading to problems (dis-eases) associated with colds and chills. It is therefore advisable to combine Moonstone with a stone that is associated with the fire element and heat-producing, or associated with stellar bodies that are heat-generating, like the planet Mars (Coral) or the Sun (Ruby).

Ideally, Moonstones should be worn set in silver, which represents the female energies.

Indian astrology considers Moonstone a sacred stone which can benefit its wearer especially if the gem weighs at least 5 and a quarter *rattis* [more than 3 carats] and is worn on the little finger of the left hand (left, again, represents the female principle).

The Moon is often associated with Shiva (the "destroyer" aspect of the threefold Divinity) who wears the crescent Moon on his forehead.

Moonstone brings clairsentience (psychic feeling), clairvoyance (psychic sight), and claircognizance (psychic knowing and clear intuition). It soothes and heals the emotions and the mind, and aids in spiritual growth and development.

Moonstone helps to soothe and balance the emotions. It assists you in mastering your emotions by bringing them under the control of your will, instead of reflexively repressing or expressing them. Moonstone represents the great Mother Goddess. Her inner strength springs from her gentleness and her ability to experience, process, and neutralize her emotions.

Moonstone helps you with discernment. "Want" and "Need" is not the same thing and the two ways of asking do not come from the same place. Moonstone can assist you in attracting those things that are "needed" in your life while helping you determine what is merely "wanted".

Some people think that Moonstone is strictly a feminine stone, because it is associated with the female principle and all things feminine, such as a woman's monthly cycle (which follows the moon when in balance). But nurture, care, and humanitarian service are not simply female attributes.

Moonstone can unblock those feelings in both men and women who are afraid to acknowledge or experience consciously how they feel on a personal and internal level. Because of its association with the water element and its "journey" across the skies, Moonstone is also considered a protective stone while traveling, especially at night or on the water.

Many people who work with Angel Cards, Crystals, meditation or any other way of accessing the Akashic Records, keep a Moonstone with them to heighten their intuition and perceptions.

Moonstone is the stone of rebirth, new beginnings and "rising again", more beautiful than ever—like the Phoenix from the flames.

It promotes happiness, grace, good fortune, hope, spiritual insight, easy childbirth, safe travel on water, new beginnings and adjusting to changes, abundance and ancient wisdom in the form of unconditional love, support, encouragement.

The German poet Rainer Maria Rilke (1875-1926) described this stone's angelic qualities perfectly when he wrote:

If the angel deigns to come
it will be because you have convinced
her, not by tears,
but by your humble
resolve to be always beginning;
to be a beginner. [6]

Numerology: 4
Zodiac: Cancer
Birth Stone: June
Chakra: Sacral, Solar Plexus, Third Eye and Crown
Element: Water
Planet: Moon

The Sixth Mermaid Crystal: Pearl

Pearls are the symbol of feminine wisdom, purity, and spiritual transformation. They support the qualities of charity, honesty, wisdom and integrity, and help bring out the best within us. Pearls provide a clear vehicle for the advancing states of wisdom, as well as a pure channel for the receipt of spiritual guidance. Pearls promote a feeling of dignity, self-acceptance and beauty.

When you wear pearls you feel calm, poised, beautiful and feminine, yet strong and rooted in your own power. Pearls not only provide a mirror in which we see ourselves, but give us insight into how we appear to others.

Pearls start out as ragged, rough grains of sand, which are transformed over time, slowly growing into an object of exceptional beauty, worth and luminescence. The Pearl shows us that mastery and overcoming of obstacles and transforming difficulties into the Path (of soul growth) produces something of great beauty and value.

Its humble origins as a grain of sand reveal to us the potential of the soul, which proceeds from the very first vibration to higher and higher stages of consciousness, which is life itself. In this way, pearls symbolize (spiritual) innocence, authenticity and a pure heart, and help us get in touch with the truth of life.

Depending on their color, pearls reflect a ray of light that supports specific qualities. The Mermaids adore pearls and work with them in all colors.

Although they are often depicted as wearing white pearls only, the Mermaids especially love black pearls, which represent wealth and abundance. It is their mission to see us all claim our divine inheritance as Children of the Tao and glorify Creation in our unique expression of abundance.

- **White:** Symbol of pure heart and mind; innocence, faith.

- **Gold and Black:** Like white; especially support wealth, abundance and prosperity.

- **Pink:** Works to heal the Heart Chakra.

Numerology: 7
Zodiac: Cancer, Gemini
Birth Stone: June
Chakra: Third Eye
Element: Water
Planet: Moon

Mermaid Stones and The Mother Goddess

As you can see, the Mermaids work primarily with the color spectrum blue, white and pink. Blue, like the ocean and the skies is a very spiritual color and connected to the throat and third eye chakra. Pink heals the heart chakra; and white combines all the colors of the visible spectrum: as a prism, it can shimmer like a rainbow.

The Mermaids love stones that have their origin in water (like pearls), near water and on islands (like larimar and pink sapphires) and are deep clear blue like the sea (blue topaz, blue sapphire and aquamarine).

They also favor stones that have a strong dolphin connection and vibrate at a higher frequency, bringing in the new age (larimar) and represent the *Yin* polarity of nature (like moonstone); the eternal feminine, the great Mother Goddess—yielding yet overcoming, fluid yet constant, life-giving and sustaining: birthing new life and destroying the old in the form of life-denying and self-destructive patterns.

The Mermaids are the Spirit of the water element and the stones they choose to work with are powerful conveyers of their message to us. The more we meditate on these stones and get to know them and their energies, the more the Mermaids will trust us and let us into their world. It is a very rewarding journey and you will discover many more Mermaid secrets along the way.

One of the most insightful books ever written about crystals and gemstones is titled *Love is in the Earth* and was written by a crystal intuitive or channel named Melody. This book, which details the metaphysical properties of the mineral plane, also touches on the fascinating topic of gemstones and their numerical vibrations.

It is important to know that you can wear certain gemstones in order to amplify the powers of your own Life Path, which is calculated in numerology by the sum of your birth date, or Expression number, which is the sum of your name value.

Once you have found your stone, you can have your Life Path Crystal set in a ring, a bracelet, a pendant, an amulet, or in earrings.

Exercise: Life Path Number

Example:

Date of Birth =

27/02/1977

Numerological Calculation =

$2 + 7 + 0 + 2 + 1 + 9 + 7 + 7 = 35$

$3 + 5 = 8$

In this example, your Life Path number is 8.

If your birth date adds up to a double-digit master number such as 11, 22, or 33, your main life mission follows the master number, while the individual numbers (1, 2, 3) and the addition of the two numbers ($1 + 1 = 2$, and so on) informs you of the attributes or directions of the master number.

Once you have calculated your Life Path number, choose the corresponding gemstone from the list included in this chapter.

Exercise: Expression Number

To do this, note down your birth name – the name that was given to you on the day of your birth.

Then find the number that corresponds to the letters of your name, one by one. Finally, add them all together.

1	2	3	4	5	6	7	8	9
A	B	C	D	E	F	G	H	I
J	K	L	M	N	O	P	Q	R
S	T	U	V	W	X	Y	Z	

Example:

Louisa	May	Hill
3 + 6 + 3 + 9 + 1 +1	4 + 1 + 7	8 + 9 + 3 + 3
—	—	—
23	12	23
—	—	—
5	3	5
	13 =	
	4	

So, in our example, Louisa May Hill's Expression number, the way she projects herself to the world at large and how she channels and focuses her Life Path, would be 4.

If you have changed your name, either by marriage or by choice at a later date, or if you permanently go by a certain name, or are known by different (nick-)names in various social circles (such as Beth at work, Betty amongst family, Liz to friends, Lily to your husband, and Elizabeth on your birth certificate) that means that the Expression of your life purpose, as articulated in different names, is changing or shifting in accordance with the situation and your assumed name.

If you hate a name that was given to you at birth, whether it's your first, middle or last name, the energy blockage related to this name and its corresponding number is always interesting to explore.

Remember, on a soul level you chose precisely the name you were born with. If you are adopted, you may have links to both your birth name and the name you were given by your adoptive parents. In any case, both were selected by you and hold important life messages for you.

You can also change your Expression number if you feel strongly that your name is not suitable for you or for the career you have chosen. In this case, you may feel that a different name would suit you better. It is always advisable to take the numerology of a name into account.

Laura Hollins was an aspiring model with much drive and potential but without any acclaim to her name when a numerologist recommended the name Agyness Deyn to her based on numerological calculations. She is now a world-famous supermodel under her "new" name.

Life Path and Expression Numbers

A short overview of the characteristics, the challenges and the life lessons of each Life Path and Expression number is given as follows:

(1) To learn through initiating, pioneering, leading, independence, success, and individuality.

(2) To learn through co-operation, adaptability, consideration, partnership, and mediation.

(3) To learn through authentic expression and verbalization, socialization, the arts, creativity, and the pure joy of living.

(4) To learn through foundation, order, service, security, expansion in a solid/structured way, and steady growth.

(5) To learn through expansiveness, adventure and the constructive use of freedom. To be a visionary.

(6) To learn through responsibility, protection, nurturing, community, balance, and empathy.

(7) To learn through analysis, understanding, knowledge, awareness, scholarship, and meditation.

(8) To learn through practical endeavors, leadership, abundance, success. Infinite potential. (The 8 sideways symbolizes infinity.)

(9) To learn through humanitarianism, giving, service, selflessness, creative expression and spirituality.

Numerology and Crystals

What follows is a breakdown of numerology numbers for each Life Path or Expression number, and the gemstones that you could wear to amplify the vibration of that gemstone. You will find that some gemstones like the Bloodstone vibrate to more than one number. Some like the Peridot vibrate to several numbers.

This is by no means a comprehensive list, but is a selection of the most common stones that are used in jewelry.

(1) Aquamarine, Beryl, Boji Stone, Copper, Cowrie, Lodestone, Mica, Muscovite, Obsidian, Sapphire, Sandstone, Turquoise

The number 1 gemstones are very distinctive and beautiful. They are individualistic, optimistic and bright but they also hide deeper secrets in their insides.

(2) Garnet, Gold, Meteorite, Moldavite, Shell, Smokey Quartz, Sugilite, Tanzanite, Tourmaline, Brown Tourmaline

The signature number 2 stone is the garnet which has always symbolized love. The smokier colored stones symbolize emotional healing.

(3) Amber, Amethyst, Aventurine, Dolomite, Herkimer Diamond, Lapis Lazuli, Morganite, Pyrite, Ruby, Pink Sapphire, Sardonyx, Sugilite, Blue Topaz

The stones for the number 3 tend to be brilliant or distinctive in some way much like the person who numerologically corresponds to this number.

(4) Ametrine, Bloodstone, Danburite, Emerald, Glass, Lead, Mochi Balls, Moonstone, Pumice, Clear Quartz, Black Sapphire, White Sapphire, Yellow Sapphire, Silver, Sodalite, Strombolite, Tiger Eye, Black Tourmaline, Zircon

Stones vibrating to the number 4 often also vibrate to the feminine principle as 4 is the number of family, foundation and healing.

aiding and guiding humans and helping them to manifest their purpose.

The word Angel is derived from the Greek word for "messenger" and the halo of an angel represents light, virtue and self-realization. To humans, angels often appear as messengers of all types of messages. More generally, angels bring the message of spirit into matter – they carry the Divine blueprint from the Creator into the manifest world.

The wings represent an Angel's role as a messenger travelling between the realms of Heaven and Earth. In reality, they are extensions of energy, which surround the entire body. An angel's aura shines so dazzlingly that it appears like a burning flame of pure white light, as bright as the Sun so that you have to avert your eyes and can barely make out the human figure at the center of this light.

If we are in perfect balance, in complete harmony, our auras are pure white, as described by Matthew in the Bible: "His face did shine like the sun, and His raiment was as white as the light." (Matthew 17:2). Like all guides, guardian angels help us to understand that we are not alone. They help us to see that we are part of a living cosmos, of which we are co-creators.

Originally Angels were not depicted with wings and the earliest example of a winged Angel in art is in a 5th century mosaic in the church of St. Prudencia in Rome. Angels in biblical and ancient non-biblical Jewish and Christian texts are portrayed as spiritual beings, superior to humans in both power and knowledge.

The Renaissance artist Raphael—whose angelic name is surely significant—painted angels in breathtaking beauty.

Angels, as Divine messengers, inspired mystics such as Emanuel Swedenborg (1688 – 1772), whose spiritual awakening and encounters with angels (as he described them) from 1746 onwards led to increased psychic and prophetic ability.

At this time in history, more and more people are now connecting with angels and have the chance to evolve as a result.

Orders of Angelic Beings

In Angelology there are nine choirs of angels divided into three groups of spheres, which are again sub-divided into three ranks each. 'Above' or 'Higher' does not mean superior, since all angels are a manifestation of the Divine. Of course, all classifications are a human construct, allowing us to give structure and order to frequencies and beings which we are unable to accurately describe with words taken from our third dimensional reality. However, the order of angels is useful in so far as it helps you to envision angels as real beings and not just marble statues. By developing a personal relationship with the angels, you start working with the celestial realms and your life becomes enriched as a result.

1st Sphere – The Heavenly Counselors

Seraphim, Cherubim and Thrones

These Angels are entirely turned towards God.

2nd Sphere – The Heavenly Governors

Dominions, Powers and Authorities

These Angels know God through their concern for the cosmos.

3rd Sphere – The Heavenly Messengers

Principalities, Archangels and Angels

These Angels oversee nations, are involved with human beings and know God through his creation.

Who are the Archangels?

Archangels are messengers from Source who guide and oversee the realm of the guardian angels and also our human physical realm. The Archangels have the magnificent ability to help each of us simultaneously while offering their protection and guidance to bring about peace on earth.

Traditionally, there are seven Archangels which each represent a color of the rainbow, a specific ray of light, but people have been divided on which angels to include in this category. The seven rainbow rays are violet, indigo, turquoise, green, yellow, orange and red. This rainbow of colors is also reflected in the "inner rainbow" of the seven major physical chakras, which range from red (base chakra) to violet (Crown chakra).

In Christianity, the seven angels that stood before God in Revelations are considered to be the Archangels. Most accounts name Michael, Gabriel, Raphael, and Uriel as Archangels while the remaining three are generally chosen from Metatron, Ariel, Zadkiel, Jophiel, Chamuel, Raguel, Nathaniel, Azrael, Haniel, Jeremiel, Sandalphon and Raziel. This circle widens because the angels reach out to us as we are opening our eyes, ears and hearts to their signs and communications. With our human senses we can feel the help, support and joy that an angelic encounter brings but we do not always know exactly which angel helped us, or how to classify them.

The angels have told me that the information on the seven Archangels, seven rainbow colors, seven days of the week, and seven major Chakras in the body relates to the third dimension. The number 7 synthesizes what is visible to us at the third dimensional consciousness level.

In reality, there are many more Archangels, but not all of them are contactable by humans yet. As our frequencies evolve and we become more spiritual, more and more light begins to fill our cells. Our bodies literally become lighter, that is, more light-filled and we seem to glow. The angels tell me that more Archangels will be revealed (that is become accessible) to humankind as we build our crystalline light bodies and raise our vibrations.

At present, there are 16 Archangels that I want to focus on, all with different aura colors, gemstones and specialties; who we can call on for help. Just visualizing the Angel's aura color around a person or object is going to protect and heal them. You can never send too much light to a person, situation or object. Angel Light is pure love so it is limitless and always beneficial.

Anyone can call on an Archangel for assistance. If you find yourself in need of help, clarity or calm or you wish to connect with an Archangel merely thinking of the Archangel's name is sufficient and all you have to do. He or She will instantaneously be called to your side. When you develop your relationship with the Archangels, you receive healings, guidance and miracles in your life. You can amplify this relationship by choosing to work with the gemstone associated with each of the 16 Archangels. You will notice that most of the names of the Archangels end in the suffix "-el", which means "in God". The names of Metatron and Sandalphon end in "-on", and they are the only Archangels (that are known at this time) that walked the earth in human form.

16 Archangels – Aura Colors, Gemstones and Specialties

I am told that as we leave the Age of Pisces with its emphasis on order, structure and systems (which is a fear-based reaction to Pisces natural free-flowing spirituality) humans will recognize that there are more Archangels and color frequencies they can evoke and call upon than previously believed. The Archangels dispense their rays generously to Earth, with the aim of helping and healing people. Every Archangel is associated with a specific color frequency which is related to His/Her attributes and area of expertise.

Of course, all Archangels can be of help with anything but if you call on an Archangel that has specialized in an area it is like calling a surgeon or a neurologist instead of a family doctor. They have the same training and level of accomplishment, but each has their own area of expertise. Like humans, Archangels are individuals and no two are exactly the same – even twins.

ARIEL

Ariel, which translates to "Lion of God", is the Master Manifester. He helps us provide for physical needs such as shelter, housing, food, clothes and so on. Ariel is the Keeper of the Sacred Wisdom and is the Angel of the Earth. He aids the environment and heals animals. Ariel is the Patron Angel of Animals.

Aura Color: Pale Pink

RAZIEL

Raziel, meaning "Secret of God", knows all the secrets and laws of the Universe. He inspires us to receive Life as a mystery so that we can be more open to new and creative ideas. Raziel heals spiritual and physical blocks to soul growth. He helps to interpret dreams and past life memories. Raziel takes your soul travelling in the dream state to reveal truths and ancient wisdom that is integrated in your subconscious and remains with you when you wake up, helping you understand "hidden", esoteric information and increase your ability to see, hear, know and feel divine guidance. Raziel can help you understand metaphysics, esoteric material, laws of manifestation, sacred geometry, quantum physics and other high-level information. He can also open you up to higher levels of psychic abilities and increase your ability to see, hear, know and feel Divine guidance; which is also called (in order) clairvoyance, clairaudience, claircognizance and clairsentience. In his role of imparting Divine secrets, Raziel can also assist you with alchemy, transformation and divine magic.

Aura Colors: Rainbow Colors
Gem: Clear Quartz

SANDALPHON

Sandalphon, who was incarnated as Prophet Elijah (Enoch's twin brother) on earth, is the Archangel of Music and Answered Prayers. Sandalphon heals aggressive tendencies. He helps with communication and expression so that you may speak your truth openly, yet your words and actions are kind and gentle although they have great (spiritual) power. When we need wisdom and clarity, we can call on Sandalphon. We are often distracted and confused and may be unable to perceive the many miracles that are happening around us at any given moment. Sandalphon can help us to see that God's miracles occur all the time, and that we have just as much right to experience them as the next person. Trust and know that your prayers are heard and answered. Things can take a while; maybe the timing is not right, or maybe your objective is ego-led and does not serve your highest good. Just trust and know that your prayers have been heard. If you are feeling impatient about a change, manifestation or occurrence in your life, ask for the peace and patience to carry you through the rough sea until your prayers are answered. Or ask to see the higher wisdom in God's plan for you. Sometimes we ask for things we want, but not necessarily need. By not getting something we believe we want, God and the angels may be protecting us and paving the way for something even better to manifest in our life. One thing is for sure: The universe *always* has our best interest at heart. Pray for guidance, and pray to follow the path that is for your highest good.

Sandalphon, like his "twin" Metatron, works with children. His specialty in this domain is bringing about the gender of the embryo.

Aura Color: Cool Turquoise
Gem: Turquoise

URIEL

Uriel, meaning "God is Light" or "Fire of God", illuminates the mind, giving rise to new thoughts, ideas and knowledge. He heals resentments and un-forgiveness. Uriel gives us insights about our life path and upcoming situations in forms of visions, "knowing" and angelic guidance. He provides us with Divine ideas and intellectual guidance and lights our pathway so we know which step to take next. Uriel oversees the element of the earth and the north. He is the Angel of Nature, Visions and Instruction and Custodian of Prophecy. Uriel serves on the sixth gold light ray of Divine service. His Twin Flame or Divine Complement is Donna Grazia –the Lady of Mercy. Uriel is the leader of the Guardian Angels. A Guardian Angel can answer the calls and earnest prayers that arise from the depths of one's soul in need.

Aura Color: Gold, Blue-Purple
Gem: Amber

Without the Akashic Records, karma and law could not exist and everything would be nothing more than a sequence of random occurrences. As we can see order, intelligence and structure in everything, from the smallest flower to the highest mountain, it follows that there is a blueprint and a plan for everything. To have a plan, one must have records of what went on before.

The purpose of the cosmic play is the universe experiencing itself. The dolphins show us how to live life—joyful, light and playful.

The Akashic Records are more than just a collection of events, they contain (or "record") every thought, word, feeling, action, and intent that has occurred at any time throughout the world. Far from a passive memory bank, the Akashic Records are interactive; constituting a summary of all our soul has ever been and learnt on its path, they have an incredible influence over our daily lives, our relationships, our feelings and belief systems, and the potentials and probabilities we attract into our lives.

Beyond that, since they store information since the beginning of time, on every soul in the cosmos, they connect each of us to one another. Every archetype, symbol or mythical story that has ever touched the human soul finds its inspiration and stimulus in the Akashic Records. Dreams, ideas and inventions originate here. If you feel magnetically attracted by someone, or instantly repelled, the information on your past experiences with these individuals is stored in the Akashic Records.

Exodus 32:32 speaks of "thy book which thou hast written". In the Old Testament, we learn that there is nothing that is not known about an individual in this cosmic book. In Psalm 139, David explains that God has written down his entire "story"— everything about him and every detail of his life, including that which is imperfect and actions yet to be performed. This "book" is not a record prepared for judgment day, as many believe. The universe is more subtle, and more benevolent, than that. Judgment day refers to every day of our lives, and everything is recorded so that the One may experience itself in all.

"I saw the dead, great and small, standing before the throne, and books were opened. Another book was opened, which is the book of life.

The dead were judged according to what they had done as recorded in the books. The sea gave up the dead that were in it, and death and Hades gave up the dead that were in them, and each person was judged according to what he had done. Then death and Hades were thrown into the lake of fire. The lake of fire is the second death. If anyone's name was not found written in the book of life, he was thrown into the lake of fire." (Revelation 20:12-15).

This means that everything we do is recorded as a vibrational imprint in the "book of life" which is shown to us, between lifetimes in the interlife, in the life review that happens once we have left the body. Of course, there is not only one moment ("day") when we are "judged" according to what we have done, but every day is a living, or an outpicturing of our thoughts, beliefs and feelings. Of course, when our life is over, the impact of all we have accomplished in this lifetime becomes the focal point of attention in the life review.

Burning in the lake of fire is a symbolism for the mighty power of the light rays of the Archangels, Angels and Ascended Masters, whose spiritual light shines so brightly that it appears as flames. This light has the power to "burn" all non-truth. Everything that is illusion will be transformed into Truth. Ultimately, we will absolve ourselves of "sin" (wrongful or mistaken thinking) by realizing Christ consciousness as later explained in the New Testament:

"Therefore, my brothers, you whom I love and long for, my joy and crown, that is how you should stand firm in the Lord, dear friends! ... Rejoice in the Lord always. I will say it again: Rejoice! Let your gentleness be evident to all. The Lord is near. Do not be anxious about anything, but in everything, by prayer and petition, with thanksgiving, present your requests to God. And the peace of God, which transcends all understanding, will guard your hearts and your minds in Christ Jesus." (Philippians 4: 1-7)

Edgar Cayce, in *Edgar Cayce on the Akashic Records*, says: "For he, man, has been made just a little lower than the angels; with all the abilities to become ONE WITH HIM! not the whole, nor yet lost in the individuality of the whole, but becoming more and more personal in ALL of its consciousness of the application of the

The "innumerable eyes" refer to a cosmic memory that "records" everything: "As ye sow, so shall ye reap" is a universal principle. Every action leads to a re-action. Every vibration we send out has an effect. Nothing is ever lost. We call this "boomerang" action (what we send out comes back to us, unfailingly) the law of karma. Karma, the law of action and effect, is a teaching mechanism and has nothing to do with low-level mechanisms of retribution, punishment or guilt. It is fair and just and reveals to us the workings of the universe in our own lives. The seeds we sow (the thoughts we think) are real, and the more water (energy[1]) we provide, the faster and bigger the manifestation—good and bad. Scientifically, every idea puts forth its own frequency and corresponding photons which "crystallize" or materialize into reality. So, there is very real and measurable evidence that thoughts—literally—create.

Consider the book in your hands right now. See the page you are reading and the words on that page. Physics says that what you are perceiving is merely a holographic blur of frequency patterns (like pebbles which create overlapping rings in a pond) that are translated into a pattern of neural stimulation, which in turn is experienced by you as the object "out there". In fact, the process of determining that the object exists in solid form occurs only in your mind's interpretation of the stimulated or activated neural pathways. When you look up at the stars, you see light that the stars sent out millions and perhaps billions of years ago. Again, what we are seeing does not actually exist as we perceive it; in actuality, we are seeing a pattern of neural stimulation created by our interpretation of the light on our retinas.

What you see, hear, taste, touch, and smell are all ultimately patterns of neuronal stimulation that is connected or corresponds to what exists "out there", but is not truly that. The frequencies that are sent out and are translated into neural stimulation by you (and your senses, brain and neuronal pathways) are, in and of themselves, colorless, textureless, and tasteless. The qualities we experience through sensory perception are created by the mind and constitute an "explicate" order or secondary reality.

---

1 *Water to the mill* is a common saying, which underlines the principle of water as "energy in action".

In this way, everything we see around us, our "solid" and dependable material reality is really only a filtered version of the ultimate unity which connects everything. That also means your "filter"—your thoughts as expressed in brain energy patterns—determines what you see. You have to believe it to see it is a scientific principle as much as a spiritual one. This filtered version of reality creates separateness because it only perceives bits and pieces of the whole at any one time. Quantum physics reminds us that if we could remove the filter, we would experience reality directly as an interference pattern in which information is distributed non-locally (instantly).

We *are* this pattern. Your hands, this paper, this ink, these words, this chair, our solar system, the entire universe; it is all a seamless, continuous extension of everything else. Quantum physics shows us that there can be no objective reality because the observer, the process of observing, and the observed become one. You are what you think.

We are all connected and therefore have a measurable effect on each other. This is the reason for people flocking around famous, successful and wealthy people. *The rich get richer* may be a cliché, and appear unjust, but it's actually a natural effect of the Law of Attraction at work. People are attracted to the frequencies of success, abundance, and attainment, because they want these qualities for themselves—which is really born on a soul level from a desire to express their Divine inheritance, and their inherent worthiness and life mission.

The Butterfly Effect

The butterfly effect is an illustrative term that encapsulates the concept of *sensitive dependence on initial conditions* in chaos theory; namely that small differences in the initial condition of a dynamic (in motion) system may produce large variations in the long-term behavior of the system. It can be compared to the "paying it forward" effect where you perform a good deed without expecting anything in return. The elevation and help given to the person you choose to help is reward enough, and you know that one good deed will cause a chain reaction and set the tone for many other things to shift in a positive direction.

Although this may appear to be a mysterious and unusual behaviour, it is exhibited by very simple systems—for example, a ball placed at the crest of a hill might roll into any of several valleys depending on slight differences in initial position. The name "butterfly effect" stems from the fact that the flutter of a butterfly's wings in South America will influence weather patterns around the world. The butterfly effect is a frequent component in fiction and movies when portraying situations involving time travel and "what if" scenarios where one storyline diverges at the moment of a seemingly minor event (such as catching a train or missing it) resulting in two significantly different outcomes (such as leaving or staying in a relationship).

You can imagine reality like a piano—composed of a series of octaves; from low to high. Intelligent Infinity (the Tao) is at the eighth density or octave and is brought into Intelligent Energy in order to communicate, express and experience itself. Every person is a single sound vibratory complex. We can use this gateway to view the present, which is not the continuum we experience but the potential social memory complex of this planetary sphere. The term we use for this is the "Akashic Records", also known as The Book of Life, or the Hall of Records.

Chapter 6

Ascended Masters

Say not, "I have found the path of the soul."
Say rather, "I have met the soul walking upon my path."
- Kahlil Gibran (The Prophet)

Who are the Ascended Masters?

The Ascended Masters guide and helps us. They are accomplished, or self-realized, souls who show us what the human soul really is. Like us, they have had human bodies. They have walked the Earth and have faced the same challenges, and more, that we face today. Through their incarnations, the many lifetimes they passed here on Earth, they fulfilled the inner calling of their God Presence day by day, embodiment after embodiment. Being in a physical body, with a third dimensional orientation, is the most difficult task a soul can venture to undertake. When the connection to Source, to the Divine Heritage is lost or forgotten, the Soul loses itself in darkness. The ego-based, limited mind takes over. We forget the Life that animates us, that makes us breathe, that lets us see, that allows our flesh and blood to vibrate.

Saint Isaac of Nineveh said:

"Be at peace with your own soul, then heaven and earth will be at peace with you. Enter eagerly into the treasure house that is within you, you will see the things that are in heaven; for there is but one single entry to them both. The ladder that leads to the Kingdom is hidden within

your soul...Dive into yourself and in your soul you will discover the stairs by which to ascend."8

Spirit is Your Origin

If you had eyes to see, in other words, if your body was the source of your sense awarenesses, you would not be able to see with your eyes closed. The physical act of having a membrane tightly in front of your sight organ when your eyes are closed would also cancel all sight activity. And yet, you dream. In other words, you do not need your eyes to see. Likewise, you do not need your ears to hear. It is the other way around. You have eyes *because* you see.

A famous Zen koan (a short question asked to induce the listener to get from linear and dualistic thinking to a place of synthesis and oneness) asks: *If a tree fell down in the wood, and there was nobody there to hear it, would there still be a sound?* Of course, the correct answer to this is *no, there is no sound if there is nobody to perceive the pressure waves in terms of sound.*

The act, or perception, of seeing came first and the eye molded itself in your physical body in response. Matter always responds to Spirit. Spirit always comes first. Spirit is the Origin and Matter is the derivative, or the reflection.

Ascended Masters have fully realized their Essence and they are liberated Beings, not bound by time and space. They mastered all the lower realms of this world, learning the lessons of Life, balancing karma, fulfilling their earthly mission and finally manifesting and becoming God in action. They have completed their mission and have realized the ultimate illusion and thus power of matter. This process is called the Ascension, the permanent integration with the Light of the own true reality, the all-powerful I AM Presence.

The Ascended Masters are showing us the Path and the Way to accomplish what they have accomplished. Our hearts and souls are one. If we keep our eyes fixed on the ultimate prize, the ultimate truth that is within us, the Divine Matrix of Our Being, then it logically follows that we are treading behind them in the footsteps they have left for us to lead the way.

The Ascended Masters guide us with the Fires of Their Hearts until the very last soul is reunited with their Source and received into the Brotherhood of Light.

Jesus the Christ: The Perfected Blueprint

Jesus came forth to reveal the Conscious Authority and Mastery that is possible for every human being to attain and express, while still here on Earth. He revealed to humankind the realm of the Ascended Masters and by His example, proved what is possible for each person. He demonstrated that we can call forth our Christ consciousness, or God-Self, and when we do this, we gain conscious control over all material manifestations, to the point of performing "miracles" such as walking on water, curing the sick and rising from the dead.

The Ascended Masters Are Real Beings

The Ascended Masters are tangible Beings of Light. They are real, visible, glorious, living and caring friends who hold such Love, Wisdom and Power that the human mind struggles to grasp its luminosity and intensity. Having conquered and gained Mastery over the Self, they now work everywhere in the universe in utter bliss, freedom and wisdom. They have recognized Illusion and have thereby gained limitless power to naturally accomplish deeds which the average individual would consider supernatural, or a "miracle". A miracle is nothing else than the Laws of the universe acknowledged, understood and applied.

Ascended Masters are Illuminated

Lumen-, lumin-, lum-, is Latin for light, shine, or source. *Illumination means shining in the light of Source.*

According to teachings of Agni Yoga, Serapis Bey also incarnated as King Numa Pompilius, as well as the philosophers Confucius, Plato and Seneca.[10]

Serapis was also embodied as Leonidas, king of Sparta. In about 480 B.C., with only three hundred soldiers, he resisted the advance of Xerxes' vast Persian army in a Herculean effort at Thermopylae. Though eventually defeated, their standing fast and fighting to the last man is celebrated in literature as the epitome of heroism in the face of overwhelming odds. Serapis Bey ascended in about 400 B.C.

In the twentieth century, the Ascended Master Serapis Bey dictated the book *Dossier on the Ascension: The Story of the Soul's Acceleration into Higher Consciousness on the Path of Initiation* (1963), a number of messages which were noted down by Mark L. Prophet. In these communications, Serapis gives profound answers to the questions of life after death. He outlines step by step how to follow in the footsteps of the adepts (East and West) who have gone before and demonstrated the potential of the human soul to us, including Jesus Christ; who have been candidates at the mystery school of Luxor, Egypt, submitting to the initiations of the Sphinx and the Great Pyramid.

Serapis teaches us how to live life to its fullest in the here and now and how to consciously ascend (accelerate) into that higher reality which is the eternal abode of the soul. His Retreat is in Luxor, Egypt and his Gift is *Working of Miracles*. The musical keynote of Serapis Bey is "Celeste Aïda" by Verdi and the keynote of his etheric retreat is "Liebestraum" by Liszt.

I received the essence "Serapis Bey" as a protective aura shield and healer from an Aura Soma practitioner who gave me a consultation when I had brain cancer for the second time. My life essence bottle and door (or guidance) to my higher self that I spontaneously picked was magenta in color and, as I later discovered, bottle number 77, my birth year.

I was told that the color magenta relates to a transpersonal life purpose (and the soul star chakra) and is associated with old souls who have completed the third dimensional life cycle and have incarnated with a vision beyond themselves. I have always strongly felt that my mission in this life is to be of service and to help people to live life authentically by the sharing of spiritual truth. My near-death experience in December 2006 confirmed this life mission.

Invocation for Wednesday

"Tenderly Beloved Presence of God, I AM a spark of the divine which is the Beloved Christ Self in my heart. I love You and adore You. I invoke the White Flame of Purity and Hope to purify me and every life I touch. You know my soul's purpose. I wish to fulfill the purpose of my existence through my manifestations and the vibrations of my own world. Please help me and guide me in living life from the heart and always expressing my life purpose according to Your highest vision. I love knowing that my life is one with the Divine Plan. Everything I think, say, or do, is in harmony and alignment with my true, spiritual self. And So It Is."

Thursday – The Fifth Ray

Thursday is represented by the Green Flame. Hilarion is Master of the Fifth Ray, the emerald green ray, of Truth, Science, Vision, Abundance and Healing. He is helping to bring in the scientific aspect of the New Age. He is particularly teaching us to use our mental powers and drops seed thoughts of the new technology and scientific ideas into receptive minds. He works with souls to help them gain mastery in the third-eye chakra and green ray qualities, including healing and the science of holding the immaculate concept. (The immaculate concept is any pure thought held by one person for another.) His gift is *Healing*. Hilarion often works together with Archangel Raphael, who also serves on the Fifth Ray.

One of the greatest masters of the Fifth Ray, the ray of Truth, is Pallas Athena. She is the Goddess of Wisdom in the Greek canon, but she is in fact an Ascended (Lady) Master. She was the Muse that inspired Francis Bacon, Shakespeare, and their circle of Elizabethan authors.

the rhythm and the application of the law through service and reverence for life.[2] Arcturus oversees the purple flame, concentrating on the scientific action of the law and the transmutative quality of freedom, while Victoria radiates the violet (orchid-colored) flame, demonstrating the compassion and love components of freedom.

Omri-Tas is the Ruler of the Violet Planet. His aura carries the violet flame and the seventh ray in such an intensity that the light extends far beyond the physical boundaries of the planet. The development and progress of the Violet Planet have served the violet flame for eons.

In past incarnations, St. Germain has embodied as the prophet Samuel, Joseph (husband to Mary, mother of Christ), Saint Alban (first martyr of Britain in the 3rd century), Merlin (alchemist, prophet and counselor at King Arthur's court) in the 5th century, philosopher and scientist Roger Bacon (1220-1292), Christopher Columbus (1451-1506), and English Renaissance philosopher Francis Bacon (1561-1626).[12] Francis Bacon, a brilliant English philosopher, politician and scientist, is widely believed to be the illegitimate son of Queen Elizabeth I. St. Germain also lived in Atlantis, where he was a High Priest in the Temple of Healing.

In *The Masters and the Path* (1925) by C.W. Leadbeater, St. Germain is named as both the "Comte de St. Germain" and the "Master Rakoczi".

St. Germain and Lady Portia have a retreat named "The Cave of Light" in the etheric realms above the northern mountain chain of India and he also gifted the retreat known as the "Cave of Symbols" over the Teton Mountains, Wyoming, USA, to the Earth and her inhabitants. Germain/ Rakoczi also has a spiritual retreat in the etheric over Transylvania, Romania.

As you can see by the Archangel that governs the seventh violet ray—Zadkiel—and his divine counterpart Holy Amethyst, the Violet Flame and St. Germain work with the powerful crystal energies of

2 The phrase "Reverence for Life" is a translation of the German phrase "Ehrfurcht vor dem Leben"—more accurately translated as "to be in awe of the mystery of life". These words came to the German doctor and philosopher Albert Schweitzer on a boat trip on the river Oguwe in Equatorial Africa, whilst searching for a universal concept of ethics for our time. He made the phrase the basic tenet of an ethical philosophy which he developed and put into practice.

the Amethyst. St. Germain and Lady Portia's key crystal is the amethyst—the stone which concentrates and holds the vibrations of the violet Ray. Amethyst is the stone of the Alchemist and the stone of the Aquarian Age. Lady Portia wears a necklace around her neck which is adorned by a large teardrop shaped amethyst, whilst St. Germain wears a square-cut amethyst fitted over a Maltese cross. Lady Portia's crystal holds the purple and gold flame while his amethyst reveals the energies of the violet planet in holographic form.

St. Germain's current role is to help bring enlightenment to humanity in order to help Earth progress to the next evolutionary level, which will make it possible for us to see higher frequencies and higher rays, which are correlated with higher states of consciousness. This mission includes guiding and teaching those currently incarnated who are working with these Rays, as well as ascended souls who have chosen to live with us here in physical embodiment at this time.

Saint Germain's role as Sponsor (Hierarch) of the Aquarian Age is to work with light-workers who invoke the violet flame to realize their God Self, live their soul purpose and ring in the golden age of Aquarius—an age of peace and enlightenment.

The angels say: *"Pierce the Violet Flame through your heart and then let go and know who you are."*

Invocation for Saturday

"Tenderly Beloved Presence of God, I AM in my Self. I am now reborn. I AM the perfect energetic blue print of my Presence, given to me by Divine Grace and Love. All my transgressions to this very moment, I sincerely regret and I invoke the Law of Forgiveness. I welcome the all-conquering powers of transformation of the Violet Flame now and forever! The Violet Flame now burns through everything that is illusion in my thinking, error in my judgment, artificial in my emotions. At the very core of my Being, where the Truth shines like a diamond, lie the gifts of Divine Life, unpolluted and pure. Now I am on the Path, I am One with All.

Arthur by the Lady of the Lake—its sparkling blade symbolizing the courage, honour and virtue that could triumphantly conquer all evil.

We sense that the characters of the Arthurian legends were real. This forms its lasting appeal, popularity and nourishment of the psyche. Subconsciously, we recognize the great spiritual truths being played out in front of us. Many of the Ascended Masters known to us today were embodied at Camelot. El Morya was King Arthur; Lord Kuthumi was Sir Parsifal; Lanello (Mark Prophet) was Lancelot; Saint Germain was Merlin; and Amerissis, the Goddess of Light, the Twin Flame of El Morya, was the Lady of the Lake.

The Angels say:

The Holy Grail of legend and myth is your very own consciousness, which you are called to purify and consecrate as the Sacred Chalice, filled with the luminous light of your innate Divinity. This is what is meant by illumination, or en-light-enment. You are to be the Holy Grail of your own God Presence.

Chapter 7

Atlantis

We don't live in a world of reality,
we live in a world of perceptions.
- Gerald J. Simmons

What is Atlantis?

The non-physical, disembodied entities (or consciousness stream) called "Abraham" inform us that the descriptions we have of Atlantis are correct and accurate. However, it is important to bear in mind that there have been thousands of "Atlantises". In other words, Atlantis is a description.

Essentially, when embodied beings like humans tap into vibrational history, they simplify it, and give it one label. In actuality, there were many places of the same description. The planet has been inhabited with those that we call "human" for millions of years. The re-alignment and re-configuration of the planet (such as pole shifts and Ice Ages) have caused many of these sorts of upheavals, disturbances and destructions. Not just one. Atlantis is real, but it is also an archetype and represents many other "lost" continents and civilizations. Bearing this in mind, we will go on to discuss Atlantis and Lemuria as the "Atlantis" and "Lemuria" that is most commonly meant when we use the names.

Atlantis Today

Stories of floods, waves of destruction, pole shifts and natural disasters have a powerful effect on the human psyche. One of the best known stories from the Bible is the tale of Noah's Ark and the Big Flood. A highly popular recent science-fiction thriller, *The Day After Tomorrow* (2004), depicted a pole shift, tornados, hurricanes, tidal waves and a coming Ice Age of planetary proportions. Modern day New York was shown as wiped out in a day; submerged under ocean water and frozen under icy snow.

The two highest grossing films ever, *Avatar* (2009) and *Titanic* (1997) depicted great, all-conquering love affairs in the midst of the highest danger, which was represented in one film by drowning (*Titanic*) and in the other (*Avatar*) as the Sons of Belial (people who have turned away from their soul values) encroaching on an idyllic, connected and conscious way of life.

These are memories of Atlantis and Lemuria drowning under the waves and the fight between good (the Children of the Law of One, who follow their souls and God) and evil (the Sons of Belial, who have become attached to, and are drowning in, matter) which are still present in every cell of the human body today. Many people living today are the reincarnations of Atlantean souls, who must now face similar temptations as before.

The Mermaids call us to remember that nothing that takes place in our soul journey is ever truly lost. Every event, thought and word is stored in the Akashic records and our own subconscious. We learn and evolve by experience, one moment at a time.

The Three Cycles of Expression

While many people nowadays perceive the "lost" civilizations of Atlantis and Lemuria as mythological, the Angelic realms teach us that humans have had three cycles or expressions of density. In this light, Lemuria was the first, Atlantis the second, and the present Earth cycle is the third cycle—the densest, or most physically-focused. Atlantis existed, it was real and we can learn many things from it.

The Mermaids want us all to learn from the Atlantean experience, for, as the Irish political philosopher Edmund Burke (1729 – 1797) said: "Those who don't know history are destined to repeat it." If we can understand the Atlantean civilization, know which pitfalls to avoid and can learn and be inspired by the Golden Age of Atlantis, it will have served its purpose.

Atlantis Reborn

"Atlantis" describes a civilization here in three dimensional reality on Earth that spanned from 200,000 B.C. to ca. 10,000 B.C. and was characterized by epochs of great heights, evolved civilizations and lived spirituality (so magnificent in fact that the period between 25,000 and 12,000 B.C. became known as the "Golden Age" of Atlantis) interspersed with periods of darkness which led to the experiment of Atlantis being terminated three times, with the last termination being final and the entire rest of the continent being submerged under water in what is now the Atlantic ocean.

Edgar Cayce said on its location:
> "The position as the continent Atlantis occupied is that as between the Gulf of Mexico on the one hand—and the Mediterranean upon the other. Evidences of this lost civilization are to be found in the Pyrenees and Morocco on the one hand, British Honduras, Yucatan and America upon the other. There are some protruding portions within this that must have at one time or another been a portion of this great continent. The British West Indies or the Bahamas, and a portion of same that may be seen in the present – if the geological survey would be made in some of these – especially, or notably, in Bimini and in the Gulf Stream through this vicinity, these may be even yet determined." (Reading 364-3)

Atlantis existed on parts of the Atlantic Ridge from about 200,000 B.C. until 10,000 B.C. Atlanteans also lived on the exposed continental shelves, during the height of the Ice Age, from about

28,000 B.C. to 10,000 B.C. and on a large island in the Caribbean now referred to as the Bahama Bank. During this time, vast expanses of water from the oceans were integrated into the snow and ice of the glaciers with the result that the Atlantic Ocean was approximately 350 feet lower than today and most of the continental shelves were above the surface. The continental shelves extend out as far as two hundred miles from the present shore lines of America and Europe. Land areas in the North Sea, the English Channel, as well as much of the Caribbean area were also above the surface of the ocean during the last half of the Ice Age.

Atlantis was a vast continent, approximately equal in size to Europe (including its Asian part) and located in the space where we now find the Atlantic ocean, hence its name. The continent of Atlantis went through three major periods of division when the mainland was divided into islands. Cayce named these as Poseidia, Og and Aryan. Edgar Cayce gives the date of the sinking of "Poseidia", as he called the last, western part of Atlantis near Bimini and Andros Island in the Bahamas, as around 10,000 B.C.

Atlanteans were gifted with many advanced psychic abilities and technologies, and later became the geographically remote yet strikingly similar civilizations of the ancient Egyptians and the pre-Columbian Americans.

The ancient Egyptians, according to Plato's *Critias,* described Atlantis as an island stretching approximately 700 km across, consisting largely of mountain ranges along the shore and in the northern regions, and "extending in one direction three thousand stadia [about 600 km], but across the center inland it was two thousand stadia [about 400 km]." This was the last, remaining part of the great continent of Atlantis.

The Azores, the Canary Islands, the Greek islands Crete and Santorini in the Aegean, the island of Cyprus off the coast of Turkey and land belonging to the Bahamas archipelago around Bimini are considered to be parts of the vast continent of Atlantis, spanning what is now the Atlantic Ocean, which used to be mountaintops and still remain above sea level.

Earth's Grid System

The Earth's grid system is constituted from ley lines and energy lines, which encircle and enfold the entire planet. Reality is a holographic grid program created by consciousness that repeats in cycles. This system can be best understood by studying Sacred Geometry. The grids are a matrix of sound, light and color through which we experience and learn. In physical reality grids are electromagnetic energy which creates polarity or duality of experience, always seeking to restore balance and forever in (spiraling) motion. Grids never stop creating programs of experience.

Timetable of Atlantis and Lemuria

This is an approximate timetable for the civilizations and events in Lemuria and Atlantis. As you can see, the two civilizations partially overlapped.[13]

1,000,000 – 800,000 B.C.	Early Lemurian Development
500,000 B.C.	Lemuria flooded by water, population scattered.
400,000 – 300,000 B.C.	Lemuria inhabited and civilization evolved.
250,000 B.C.	Second Lemurian catastrophe (possibly volcanoes and/ or meteorites)
200,000 B.C.	Early Atlantean cultures appeared.
80,000 B.C.	First Atlantean disaster; final submergence of Lemuria.
28,000 B.C.	Second Atlantean disturbance; recorded in the Bible as the "Great Flood".
10,700 B.C.	Final destruction and sinking of Atlantis

to those they performed in Atlantis. They would undergo initiations similar to those they undertook in Atlantis which would re-awaken their memories and reveal to them who they are (at a soul-level) and what their role is today. They feel or know that they have promised to return to help souls become initiates of the sacred path once again as the planet moves to the next vibrational level.

Plato on Atlantis

In the first historically recorded document on Atlantis, in 350 B.C., the Greek philosopher and scholar Plato wrote about a country he called Atlantis. Drawn from accounts by the ancient Athenian lawmaker Solon, Plato describes Atlantis, before it sank in about 10,000 B.C., as an extensive, inhabited island in the Atlantic Ocean, located "outside the Pillars of Heracles" (which we now call the Straits of Gibraltar). It is important to note that Plato did not create a mythology when he wrote of Atlantis; rather, he reiterated a tradition which had been handed down to him as "historical". Plato addresses Atlantis specifically in two of his dialogues, *Timaeus* and *Critias*.

In Plato's unfinished *Critias*, Zeus, the chief of the Gods, had just decided to convene a council of the gods to determine the fate of the Atlanteans. We, the reader, have already been informed of the result of that council from the *Timaeus*. Plato writes that after suffering tremendous earthquakes and floods, the island of Atlantis, with all her war-loving, aggressive and vengeful inhabitants (whom Cayce called the "Sons of Belial"), was destroyed, disappearing beneath the waves of the Atlantic Ocean.

Plato describes the Atlanteans as highly spiritual beings in the beginning, fully conscious of the fact that they were consciousness projecting itself into form; but slowly the God-Self aspect of their being, which shone so brightly at first, became diluted by the baser and denser human (or animal) elements of their nature, which began to take over. The Atlanteans eventually became greedy, materialistic, and war-mongering.

In Greek mythology, King Cronos ruled during a Golden Age, introduced agriculture, and established cities and law. The Golden Age was a time of abundance and peace.

Hesiod, in 735 B.C., who was quoted by Plato, writes about the Golden Age of Cronos in his *Theogeny*, a work about the Ancient deities; but in *Works and Days*, where he is describing humankind, he resorts to a different set of terms.

He portrays humankind as a series of "races", beginning with a Golden Race, but upon the demise of the Golden Race, a lesser (lower vibration, or denser) Silver Race was then created. Later, he writes, followed the Bronze Race (the race of Heroes) and finally the inferior Iron Race. He informs us that the original Golden race "lived in the time of Cronos during the Golden Age". This is a description of the soul's, or Spirit's, descent into matter.

Since these are oral traditions carried down by the ancient Greeks, mostly in ballads and epic poems, no time frame is given; but the sequence as set out is certainly indicative of the gradual deterioration of mankind parallel to Plato's depiction of the fate of the Atlantean people.

The gradual deterioration referred to here can be read as a descent into matter, a densification of the physical body, which is accompanied by materialism and a forgetting of one's spiritual origins. There is an overall plan to the soul's development or evolution and it is materially lived out for us—externalized—for all to follow.

Cayce relates the soul's descent, or projection, into matter like this:

"It is seen that individuals in the beginning were more of thought forms than individual entities with personalities as seen in the present, and their projections into the realms of fields of thought that pertain to a developing or evolving world of matter, with the varied presentations about same, of the expressions or attributes in the various things about the entity or individual, or body, through which such science—as termed now, or such phenomena as would be termed—became manifest."[15]

Lemuria. Other names mentioned are Mu (the ancient Motherland), and Zu; while Oz refers to modern-day Peru.

The different names used refer to various civilizations and also to provinces of the continent, or to portions left after a major break-up of the land. Lemuria survives in the mythology of Hindus and Australian aborigines, Polynesians and Native Americans.

According to Cayce, Lemuria—like Atlantis—was a highly developed civilization that collapsed around 80,000 BC. Survivors of the catastrophe fled to countries like China and Japan (in modern terminology) when Lemuria sank into the sea.

This event, and the story of Lemuria, survives in the mythology of Hindus and Australian aborigines, Polynesians and Native Americans. Hopi legend informs us that: "Down on the bottom of the seas lie all the proud cities, the flying *patuwvotas*, and the worldly treasures corrupted with evil."

Lemuria, a continent that existed even prior to Atlantis, was stretched out in the Pacific Ocean and left its traces on what is now known as the Easter Islands. In Cayce's words: "The Andean, or the Pacific coast of South America, occupied then the extreme western portion of Lemuria [when] a portion of Lemuria began its disappearance."

Lemuria was a civilization which flourished on this planet at a time when humankind was aware of its spiritual nature, and knew that it was spiritual consciousness having a physical experience, not the other way around, as is too often the case today. We are not bodies experiencing transcendent states (in dreams, near-death experiences or out of body experiences) and not even bodies with a soul. We are spirit projecting itself into matter.

Physically, it is believed that Lemuria existed largely in the Southern Pacific, between North and South America in the East, and Asia and Australia in the West. At the zenith of its civilization, the Lemurian people were both decidedly evolved and exceedingly spiritual.

The Early Lemurians

In the very beginning, Lemurians were thought forms who desired a dense body in order to experience physicality, sense awareness and matter. They wanted to come into matter to create, experience and add to the experience of the whole. The first Lemurians were "entities" (souls) that projected themselves mentally into a denser vibration.

They had pliable, jelly-like bodies and were extremely light and etheric. They were also very tall and could change their looks and objects at will, by just thinking about the change, a skill we now call psychokinesis (affecting material objects with the mind).

The original height of mankind on this planet was approximately 12 feet tall. By the time Lemuria sank, the Lemurians were reduced to 7 feet in height. Body size on our planet has further decreased since those times. Humans nowadays are mostly 5 – 6 feet tall with some variation at both ends. As our civilization evolves, body height will be restored. Even now, people on this planet are much taller than they were only 100 years ago.

The temperature of the planet, the atmosphere, the light and the orbits of the other planets were very different then. The first Lemurians were androgynous, neither male nor female. Some of the souls came from the "Red Planet" (Mars). Some of the souls came from other stars, such as the Pleiades and Sirius, and projected into physical form on Earth.

Some groups chose water, some the plant kingdom, the mineral kingdom, or the animal kingdom as life forms into which to project. Greater experiments were possible within the animal kingdom as this realm allowed for longer life spans and greater mobility. The Earth nourished (now mythological) species at that time which included giants (actually, we would consider the Lemurians who stood 10 – 12 feet tall "giants" from our point of view) and elves. The souls from Lemuria who wanted to continue their soul journey on this planet eventually went on to become the Atlanteans.

Lemurians very slowly lowered their vibrations so that they became denser and more material as time went on. This gradual change also came with a rigidity and stiffness they had not known thus far. Early Lemurians had to get used to having a physical vehicle for the soul, and the vulnerability and frailty of the body is still a major source of fear for humans to this day.

Twin Flames

The first Lemurians were hermaphrodites who communicated by mental telepathy through the use of the "Third Eye". When humans lost contact with their spiritual nature and descended ever further into matter, the Third Eye atrophied and became the pineal gland still found in modern humans. Finally, the ever-increasing density of matter caused a breaking apart of the One into two halves, which had the same soul blueprint but were distinct entities from now on.

The two soul halves are called Twin Flames. They are literally the same soul, with the same Divine blueprint, split into two. That means that each one of us without exception has a soul complement that exists. In other words, *we are never alone.*

The other soul may be in physical form and enter our life at some point (and the recognition will definitely strike us like lightning) or they may not meet us in physical form in this life while they learn their soul lessons and progress in different worlds or realms at the moment until the moment we are ready to reunite.

The Origin of Sex

The polarity in physicality, in the form of male and female, instigated the era of sexual reproduction. Two distinct sexes emerged from one being. This event has been described as "the fall of man" and from the time of their physical split, male and female would strive to come together as one body through physical union.

Physical union without love is a losing of the self in matter, sense awareness and short-lived pleasure. If it is practiced for this end only it can lead to compulsive behaviour, negativity, and depression. What we are looking for on a soul level is a partner who will complement us on all levels – spiritually, mentally and emotionally as well as physically. The act of reunion in the flesh is an outward act of inner, spiritual, communion.

The Law of One

There was a soul (or an "entity", as Cayce called it) among the Lemurian princesses who established the teachings of the Law of One which taught humans to practice unity consciousness and recognize their spiritual nature and their Higher (God) Self. Eventually, as this was more and more neglected and forgotten, destructive forces in Lemuria followed ego-based agendas based on the gratification of selfish motives due to (voluntary) separation from divine love.

Invocations of the sacred flame in the heart—the divine spark of Christ consciousness that connects every soul to God—were offered by priests and priestesses on Lemuria in the spirit of the science of the Logos; which is the science of harnessing the light of God through the use of the spoken word to effect positive changes in the self and in the world. The throat chakra holds to power of the Logos and when it is dedicated to the affirmation of the Word of God, it becomes an instrument of divine manifestation; as it is written: "By thy words thou shalt be justified, and by thy words thou shalt be condemned."[18]

The perversion of this science in the practice of black magic occurred later, in the last days of Lemuria, and was the cause for the destruction of the temples and the cataclysm which eventually drowned the continent. The Easter Island statues are the traces that remain and mark the site of the wars that made the Earth quiver and tremble in those horrendous days.[19]

The Human Challenge

The Bible refers to this evolved human (*homo sapiens* in five manifestations) as the first man of earth, as "Adam". When souls incarnate into physical form, they bring the divine consciousness (the breath of life, or the Spirit) in with it. This divine consciousness is referred to as the "Christ Consciousness", or the "Buddha Nature" or the "super-consciousness". Christ consciousness was not manifested only in the personality known as Jesus.

The fruition of this seed, or promise, means that a person has attained a complete human-divine unity. This human-divine unity has been attained by many people thus far – one person who came to demonstrate this principle in all its inherent glory and fulfillment was Jesus; hence his by-name, the Christ.

The challenge for the soul intertwined with matter is to overcome the base or animal nature of the human body which can lose its very essence, or soul, in sense gratification. It turned out to be possible for physicality to become so dominant in the mind of humans that they forgot their spiritual origins and worshipped matter because they believed it to be the only reality. Matter became their master.

The ultimate challenge for those on Earth is the dis-entanglement of the soul from matter and the honoring of both—success is measured by the amount of joy that is experienced, which is a direct indicator of the extent that the soul is as free in the body as out of it. Only when the body stops being a hindrance to the free expression of the soul is the cycle of physical incarnations complete. This is the condition of having a perfect unity of the human with the divine.

The Dolphin Code

At the high point of their civilization and when spirituality shone as the central light, Lemurians were telepathically linked to the Dolphins. Their tones were called "Dolphin Codes". I will discuss dolphins and their special connection to mermaids and the ancient civilizations of Lemuria and Atlantis in more detail in the chapter on Mermaids and Dolphins.

Lemuria and Atlantis

Atlantis and Lemuria existed partially at the same time. In general, the more scientific and rational group inhabited Atlantis, while Lemuria was inhabited by individuals that were more artistically and spiritually inclined. Of course, both ways of being, which can also be described as an emphasis on the left brain hemisphere (Atlantis) and the right brain hemisphere (Lemuria), manifested in both cultures. When harmony and balance between the two poles (left brain-right brain; masculine-feminine, yin-yang) was accomplished, the result was peace, harmony and a whole, rounded soul and society. In the Golden Age of Atlantis, this state of balance and harmony was made manifest and the potential and possibility for humans to attain this way of life again has never been greater.

In Atlantis, the souls that focused on ethics, values and spirituality were called the Children of the Law of One. The darker side of human nature, with its emotions of greed, lust, envy and revenge was made manifest in the Sons of Belial. These two groups were very differently focused. While the Children of the Law of One never lost sight of their true Source and Being and always retained the awareness that they were spiritual Beings having a physical human experience, the Sons of Belial forgot the knowledge of their origin and "drowned" in the baser instincts of the human mind and the body's animal nature. The result was war, destruction, poverty (spiritual and material), cruelty, and a complete disregard for life. Eventually, large-scale experiments which took place in Atlantis caused the ultimate destruction of both civilizations due to dramatic geo-physical dislocations.

The Lemurian Age took place approximately between the years 1,000,000 BC to about 80,000 years ago. Until the sinking of the continents of Lemuria and later of Atlantis, there were seven major continents on this planet. The lands belonging to the gigantic continent of Lemuria included lands now under the Pacific Ocean as well as Hawaii, the Easter Islands, the Fiji Islands, Australia and New Zealand, and also lands in the Indian Ocean and Madagascar. The Eastern coast of Lemuria also extended to California and part of British Columbia in Canada.

For a very long time before the fall in consciousness, the Lemurians lived in a fifth dimensional frequency or dimension, and were able to switch back and forth from fifth to third dimensional consciousness at will, without any problem. The adjustment in consciousness could live life in freedom, love and joy we start to raise our frequencies to those of Lemuria.

Lemuria has never been completely destroyed as it is perceived at present. It still exists in a fifth dimensional frequency, not visible to our third dimensional vision and perception. As the veil between those dimensions continues to become thinner, you will see Lemuria, in a not too distant future, in new splendor and glory in a very physical and tangible way.

As you open yourself up to a higher conscious way of living and purify yourself of all distorted and erroneous belief systems you have embraced in the last millennia, you will be able to perceive your beloved Motherland, once again, and eventually be allowed to step into her wondrous beauty and splendor while you create a Golden Age of life on earth. You will be invited to, once again, join very tangibly in this place of paradise. When Lemuria was destroyed and "lost" to the third dimension, the civilization and what it represented to this planet was lifted into a higher, fifth dimensional frequency. There, Lemuria continued to thrive and evolve to the level of perfection and beauty it has now attained in conjunction with those souls who were able to join Lemuria's frequency at the time.

EXERCISE: LEMURIAN ROYAL WISDOM

If this information brings tears to your eyes and opens your heart to heal the hurts, heartaches and pains that have been buried for so long, *give in and let it flow*. Give yourself permission to grieve and let the flow of your tears bring healing to every part of your being. Allow yourself to open and fully experience the memory, images and emotions. Feel your breath, breathe slowly and consciously and accept it fully. Embrace your heart with the breath. Breath by breath, step by step, you will heal your heart. True healing comes from within. As you breathe, with every breath you take, your God-Self heals your scars forever.

Ask the Angels and Mermaids to assist you in revealing the records that are holding you back from manifesting your new glorious reality.

In your daily meditation, we ask you to do this work faithfully until you feel a sense of completion. Connect with us and with our Love, heart to heart. You may ask for our guidance and support, and we will be by your side as you undertake this most important inner work. Together, we can manifest a Golden Age; a civilization that has fully opened and healed the heart chakra, and a vibration that pulses with the Heart of the Tao. As the deep-seated hurt is lifted, your cells will be filled with more and more light and you will feel that you are walking very lightly on the earth. When the pain-body disappears, the veils fall away and you are able to see who you really are. In this way, you make the quantum leap into your full spiritual, emotional and physical rebirth.

The New World is about to be born. Many of us have learned our lessons of Love and the new Golden Age, the lost paradise, is about to manifest again. The Soul that remains faithful to the Light and the sacred calling is lifted up to the 5th dimension at the time of ascension.

are so smart that they should be treated as "non-human persons".[20] Studies into dolphin behaviour have highlighted how similar their communications are to those of humans and that they are more intelligent than chimpanzees. This information has been backed up by anatomical research showing that dolphin brains have many key features associated with high intelligence.

According to zoologists at Emory University in Atlanta, Georgia, who have used magnetic resonance imaging (MRI) scans to map the brains of dolphin species and compare them with those of primates, many dolphin brains are larger than our own and second in mass only to the human brain when corrected for body size.

The neuroanatomy suggests psychological continuity between humans and dolphins and has profound implications for the ethics of human-dolphin interactions. The studies show how dolphins have distinct personalities, a strong sense of self and can think about the future.

Research has also shown that dolphins are "cultural" animals, meaning that new types of behaviour can swiftly be picked up by one dolphin from another. A study conducted by Hunter College, City University of New York, showed that bottlenose dolphins could recognize themselves in a mirror and use it to inspect various parts of their bodies, an ability that had been thought limited to humans and humanoid apes.

Other research has shown dolphins can solve difficult problems, while those living in the wild co-operate in ways that imply complex social structures and a high level of emotional sophistication.

Dolphin Communication

Dolphins emit short pulses of sound from the oily melon, a fatty area just below the blowhole. Similar to the orientation vocalizations of a bat, these pulses, or clicks, return as echoes when the sound bounces off objects in the dolphin's course. These echo frequencies are used by dolphins to navigate the waters and to locate food, which ranges from fish and squid to shrimp.

Always intent on helping humans, dolphins use their skills to assist fishermen. An interesting collaboration between humans and dolphins has developed in Laguna (Brazil). A pod of Bottlenose Dolphins drive fish towards fishermen who remain close to the beach in shallow waters. When one dolphin rolls over, the fishermen know that this is a sign to throw out their nets. The dolphins then feed on the escaping fish. The dolphins were not trained to perform this task. Amazingly, the cooperation between dolphin and fishermen has been recorded as far back as 1847.

Dolphins also produce whistling sounds when they are excited or communicating with other dolphins. These sounds arise from the larynx.

Swimming and Breathing

Dolphins, like whales, breathe through a blowhole at the top of the head. As they travel, they break surface about every two minutes to make a short, explosive exhalation, followed by a longer inhalation before submerging again.

Their tail, like that of other aquatic mammals, strokes in an up-and-down motion, with the double flukes driving the animal forward; the flippers are used for stabilization. Dolphins are superbly streamlined and can sustain speeds of up to 30 km/h (up to 19 mph), with surges of more than 40 km/h (more than 25 mph). Their lungs, which are adapted to resist the physical challenges created for many animals by rapid changes in pressure, enable them to dive to depths of more than 300 m (1000 ft).

Dolphins in Mythology

Dolphins appear in the myths and legends of many cultures. In Hindu mythology, the Ganges River Dolphin is associated with Ganga, the deity of the Ganges river. The dolphin is said to be among the creatures which heralded the goddess' descent from the heavens. Her mount, the *Makara*, is sometimes depicted as a dolphin.

Dolphins also appear in several Greek myths, or stories, always as bringers of help and support to humankind. The Greek traveler and geographer Pausanias, who lived in the 2nd century A.D., in *The Description of Greece*, talks about Phalanthus, a character who was brought safely to shore (in Italy) on the back of a dolphin.

Likewise, the poet Arion is said to have been rescued from drowning and carried safely to land by a dolphin, at Cape Taenarum, now called Cape Matapan, a peninsula which forms the southernmost area of the Peloponnese in Greece. In Pausanias words:

"Among other offerings on *Taenarum* is a bronze statue of Arion the harper on a dolphin. Herodotus has told the story of Arion and the dolphin, as he heard it, in his history of Lydia. I have seen the dolphin at *Poroselene* that rewards the boy for saving his life. It had been damaged by fishermen and he cured it. I saw this dolphin obeying his call and carrying him whenever he wanted to ride on it."

A temple dedicated to Poseidon, the god of the sea, contained a statue of Arion riding the dolphin as a prominent feature. Dolphins were considered the messengers of Poseidon (and the ocean), and sometimes performed favors for him.

Aphrodite, Apollo, and the Sacred Dolphin

Dolphins were sacred to both Aphrodite, the Greek goddess of love, and Apollo, the Greek/Latin god of truth and the sun (which represents spiritual light), whose familiar or special animal is a dolphin.[21]

Aphrodite was born from the sea and retained close connections with it even when in fully human form again. Legend tells us that the goddess of love, Aphrodite, rose from the waves at Cyprus, an island in the far east of the Mediterranean.

Mark Anthony is claimed to have given Cyprus to Queen Cleopatra of Egypt as a lover's gift and King Richard the Lionheart was married on Cyprus. Steeped in the legends and mythology of the Mediterranean, Cyprus is a place that still has all the intrigue and mystery of those ancient days.

Aphrodite's fish attributes were transferred to her escorts, the Tritons, and less often, the female Tritonids. Aphrodite was also a fertility goddess, and the goddess of sailors and sea voyages.

Her companion, like Apollo's, was the sacred dolphin. Aphrodite subsequently was named Venus in Rome.

Apollo's first achievement was to kill the dragon (or giant serpent) Pytho, which protected the sanctuary of Pytho from its lair next to the Castalian Spring at Delphi. Here it stood guard while the *Sibyl* inhaled the trance inducing vapors from an open chasm while she gave out her prophecies.

The monstrous beast *Pytho* was the son of Gaia (Mother Earth, the primordial deity) however, and to make amends Apollo had to serve king Admetus for nine years as a cowherd.

Upon completing his service, he returned to Pytho in the guise of a dolphin, arriving at the shore with priests from Crete.

Apollo's title *Delphinios*, meaning dolphin, is likely the origin of the name Delphi and its oracle.

Dionysos, Dolphins, and Self-Knowledge

Emphasizing the benevolence, generosity and abundance that surround dolphins, the Greek philosopher Aristotle, in his *History of Animals*, wrote: "In the seas between Cyrene and Egypt there is a fish that attends on the dolphin, which is called, the *dolphin's louse*. This fish gets exceedingly fat from enjoying an abundance of food while the dolphin is out in pursuit of its prey."

Greek mythology also tells how the god Dionysos was once captured by Etruscan pirates who mistook him for a rich prince they could exchange for ransom. After the ship set sail, Dionysos invoked his divine powers, causing vines to overgrow the ship where the mast and sails had been. He then turned the oars into serpents, thereby so terrifying the sailors that they jumped overboard. Dionysos however took pity on them and transformed them into dolphins so that they would spend their lives providing help for those in need.[22]

Mystical understanding tells us that the "intoxication" displayed by Dionysos, the Greek god of wine, theatre and fertility, can be read as drinking from the cup of self-knowledge, which transforms the person from an ordinary being into a spiritually aware beacon of light.

In this way, you become "intoxicated" with life because you realize its deeper purpose and nature. The wine in the chalice represents a higher spiritual truth; just as Jesus transformed water (ordinary consciousness) into wine (Christ consciousness).

Dolphin Truth

The dolphins say: "Once you have accepted yourself as a spiritual being with a divine mission of service, love and joy, you start to shine with beauty."

The dolphins show us that when you love and enjoy what you do, abundance is a natural by-product of that feeling of immersion, timelessness and pure joy. You *know* you have found your life's purpose when you feel like this. You then also naturally become more attractive to others, who want to be near you, and be elevated by your embrace of life.

Dionysos, the Mermaids and the Dolphins all teach us the same thing: Love what you do, immerse yourself in it with total joy and abandon so that you appear intoxicated with the sheer exhilaration, pleasure and beauty of life. In this way, you become naturally magnetic and attractive to those around you who see your light, your authentic self, shine.

The Dolphin's Mission

Dolphins appeared in the oceans of planet Earth to assist humanity during these times of great changes and evolution into higher vibrations of Consciousness. They are experts in this field.

Their assignment comprises many tasks. Dolphins serve as examples of harmonious living amongst many oceanic species. They use the spiritual powers of their mind and higher awareness to continue to exist on planet Earth with great joy, playfulness and appreciation. They own no possessions and yet they have all that they need to live a healthy, active and creative life.

In addition, they use their individual and group energy to heal and to correct imbalances created on Earth. They help people physically, emotionally, mentally and spiritually to find more constructive and beneficial ways of living on Earth while helping the Earth to sustain life and remain an integral part of the solar system.

Dolphin Healing

Many people have swum in the ocean environment with these highly intelligent and spiritually aware entities. Their testimony of healing, joy, and gratitude conferred to them by the dolphins is striking. As people learn to respect and love the dolphins, they are able to understand other life forms originating on diverse planets who are also in contact with us in various environments.

The dolphins are on this planet to help us and they accomplish this through the frequencies of love, joy and harmony. They send these frequencies into the water, using sonar and sound, and charge the water that swirls around them. In this way, they create a field of harmony similar to that of chanting monks, crystal bowls or blossoming flowers. Scientists now know that the emotional changes effected by dolphin therapy (which last much longer than the "high" experienced from the release of endorphins, the body's natural opiates) can initiate a cascade of health-enhancing hormonal and physiological changes.

In addition, they affect our bodies when we are in the ocean with them, by helping us to elevate our consciousness to access streams of superior wisdom, stimulating dormant parts of our human brain and awakening innate knowledge and memories of our connectedness with higher consciousness.

While swimming in the ocean with the dolphins, we learn to access these unaware, or sleeping, aspects of our spiritual selves by accepting the initiation into the loving, joyous, melodious energy they grant us.

you rising and standing in your own power. The time is near when you will all see as we see. Life is so much fun when you see with our eyes!"

Chapter 10

Soul Mates and Twin Flames

The moment you have in your heart this extraordinary thing called love
and feel the depth, the delight, the ecstasy of it, you will discover that for
you the world is transformed.
- Jiddu Krishnamurti

Manifesting My Soul Mate

I met my soul mate following the divine law of manifestation. I did not know it at the time, but I followed the exact guidelines, rules and preparations given to manifest exactly what is desired, even if it seems completely unrealistic and unachievable by human means. My relationships up to then were passionate, intense, consuming yet also chaotic, tangled, and—ultimately—unsatisfying. Whatever it was I was looking for, I seemed unable to find it. Then, on New Year's Eve of the year 1998, I made a resolution.

I was attending a two-day long residential rebirthing course based on the technique of holotropic breathing which involved many sessions of soul work and clearing followed by expressing the journey we had been on in painting. Holotropic Breathwork is a form of breath work developed by the Russian scientist Stanislav Grof, M.D., Ph.D. and his wife Christina Grof, which allows access to non-ordinary states of consciousness. Holotropic breathing shows similarities to Rebirthing Breathwork, but was developed independently.

Holotropic Breathwork is seen as an approach to self-exploration and healing that integrates insights from modern consciousness interested, I stood firm in my resolve not to get caught up in another relationship for co-dependent or needy reasons. I just knew in my heart that this was not my soul mate. I was going to wait.

Over the course of the next few months, I met a few more men who were interested in a relationship with me, but I never felt that deep connection, or a spark with any of them, even though they outwardly fit the bill—educated, good-looking, and successful. I stayed single.

Then summer finally came and at the beginning of June I flew from Frankfurt, Germany to Manchester, England. I then took a train, a bus and a taxi to get to my final destination; a large, old, rambling building (a former priory) housing about 100 residential Buddhists (ordained and lay practitioners) in a small village in the Lake District in Cumbria. I really enjoyed the calm and quiet of my small room in a wing of the main building.

The complex was vast and contained many old buildings; including towers, spires and many acres of parks and gardens leading down along a pebbled path to a beach, where one could stand at the shore and gaze out over the sea.

It also contained a new Buddhist temple on site which was designed by an architect and is called the "World Peace Temple" and containing eight sacred symbols (umbrella, fish, vase, flower, conch, knot, victory banner and wheel) which represent the steps on the path to enlightenment.

In this magical surrounding, I spent my days walking, socializing, volunteering, meditating in the *gompa* (Tibetan for meditation room), doing *pujas* (chanting ceremonies), sharing food afterwards, and just having a wonderful time. I met many people who were dedicated to spiritual evolvement, and were very serious about their practice. Again, there were several men who showed an interest in a relationship; who took me on moonlit walks to the beach and all-around did their best to get me to feel the spark they obviously felt.

Yet, during the months of June and July I still did not meet my soul mate. Something was always missing; the feeling of instant recognition, the irresistible pull, the deeper meaning. I did not expect my soul mate to be perfect—we are all human after all—but I knew deep down that I would know him when I met him. Sometimes it felt like driving at the speed of 180 mph and not being able to take an exit and turn away from the course that was mapped out. The conviction, the *knowing*, deep inside me was something I just could not escape or deny; even if I tried.

All relationships have a spiritual dimension and we learn from every relationship we have. Soul mates are not unique to a person; we each have several soul mates—people we have spent lifetimes with in close company; as brothers and sisters, husband and wife, or parent and child. Even a close family friend, a godfather or godmother, a cousin, a grandparent or a friend, mentor or associate we seem to just "get" can be a soul mate. Twin flames are different from soul mates in the fact that we each only have one Twin Flame—the other half of our soul—and as such a Twin Flame is unique to each of us.

Twin flames were created when the soul split into two poles, two modes of expression; male and female, or yin and yang. We are all on a journey to reunite with our Twin Flame and will not feel completely "whole" until we have found the other part of us.

To do this successfully, we are all on a journey back to Source; meaning that we are all on the path of enlightenment which will integrate all parts of us and make us whole in the Self, at which point we can reunite with our Twin Flame, who is on the same soul journey as we are.

We do not always incarnate (come into a body) at the same time as our Twin Flame. When this happens, they may guide us from non-physical and teach us lessons of soul growth from there. We also each have to experience both poles, both modes to be whole; so we each incarnate as both man and woman in different lives. The soul often has a tendency towards one mode of expression or the other, and will incarnate more frequently as a male or a female; if this is the case with you, you will feel it, but it does take both sides of the coin to be experienced for the Self to become whole.

Your Twin Flame will undergo separate lifetimes and experiences and hold different memories from you; so you will not be the same, as you might expect from the other half of your own soul. But your experiences will match and complement each other in wondrous and miraculous ways. It is important to develop the Self because your soul is like a gift to your soul mate or Twin Flame; whatever you bring to the relationship provides the platform to be built upon; or the garden to be tended. The state of your soul is the bouquet of flowers you bring to a relationship.

Exercise: Reflection on the Bouquet of the Soul

Think about the bouquet of flowers you bring to your Twin Flame. You have got to hold the vision, keep the faith, *know* that the universe is bringing you exactly what you are expecting and allowing into your experience. But you also have to be ready to meet your soul mate, or Twin Flame. Love is always a two way street. You cannot expect the other person to put in all the work. Your vibrations have to match to be attractive to each other. This works best if you both love something higher than each other—God, as expressed through your own soul, in your God Self. Only then can you truly grant each other the freedom necessary to grow and evolve.

Try to see yourself objectively. See the other person's side. If you were in a relationship with yourself, what would you see?

Make a note of your strong points. Notice your weaker areas and resolve to work on the traits you do not want to add to your bouquet. Nobody expects you to be perfect but if the bouquet is to look fresh, beautiful and appealing, you need to work at it. Nobody else can "fix" you; or provide all that you need. Nobody can be with you day in, day out—lifetime after lifetime. This is your soul, and nobody else's; you have been gifted with it to take good care of it, develop it and enjoy it. Make it a wonderful temple to rest in.

As Kahlil Gibran so eloquently says in this poem about marriage and partnership, there have to be spaces for individuality to be fulfilled:

"But let there be spaces in your togetherness, let it rather be a moving sea between the shores of your souls. Fill each other's cup but drink not from one cup. (...) And stand together, yet not too near together: For the pillars of the temple stand apart; and the oak tree and the cypress grow not in each other's shadow."[25]

Make no mistake, you can have a rocky, argument-fuelled relationship even with a soul mate, and your relationship may even end in a split or a divorce; but the time you spent together provided a learning experience for you both and by building on this soul growth and by discovering what you do not want equally shows you what you *do* want.

Nothing is ever a failure, or a mistake; everything happens for a reason, and the "wrong" roads and turnings turn out to be necessary and valuable in the end.

But, everything you experience will build on your point of attraction in the new, so it is always a good idea to work on yourself first—which is really the only thing you have influence over anyway. As you are a magnetic being, and cannot help but think and thereby create and attract, you might as well think in ways that are constructive and helpful; and that will manifest what you want to experience, rather than an inferior version of it.

After you have finished your own inventory; make a list of all the points you want in a mate. If you are in a relationship right now, think about what you want from this relationship. Do not censor yourself and do not leave anything out. The universe does not judge.

Make sure that this is *your* vision, and not a reality borrowed from someone else. Remember, your authentic self knows exactly what you need and it will send you messages in form of dreams, images, symbols, books and signs.

When you have made your list, read it often. Adjust it if you like. Know and expect that you will meet this person. It is only a matter of time.

Meeting My Soul Mate

Finally, in the second week of August, the time came for me. I had waited almost eight months to meet my soul mate, the one relationship that would be worth it; and I was getting pretty impatient. The summer was drawing to a close and I would have to fly back to Germany soon to resume my medical studies to become a doctor. The international meditation course was in full swing. Almost a week of it had already passed, and there was just one week left of it.

I just could not shake the feeling that I would meet my soul mate at this event; and, as much as I tried to convince myself that I would be alright if it did not happen at this time and I would have to wait a while longer, I felt quite despondent at the idea. It didn't seem right somehow. It was as if I had read the ending to a book and knew the heroine would meet the hero and they would live happily ever after; but now I was back stuck at the beginning of the novel, knowing what was to happen, but without any idea how it was to come to pass.

One sunny day at lunchtime, I was sitting on the grass outside a marquee which had been erected on the grounds to house the many tables and chairs that were needed at mealtimes for all the visitors in attendance. I was idly waiting for my lunch round with a few friends, when a chair was pulled up and a voice said, confident and cheerfully, "So, who are you then?" I looked up and stared right into the dark blue eyes of a handsome young man with dark brown floppy hair, eccentric but stylish clothing and a nice grin on his face.

I was slightly taken aback by his familiarity and confidence, but something inside me leapt up and whispered in my ear: "This is him!" I half wanted to yield to the voice and believe in the miracle that was unfolding before my eyes but a more cautious voice whispered: "What if he's an adrenaline or relationship junkie who chases all the girls just to boost his ego?"

It took some convincing, but I soon saw that Charles—as he was called—was sincere and exactly what I had resolved to manifest all those moons ago. After the international meditation course ended, he invited me to come to France with him, where his parents owned a house. I had known him for a matter of days but I said yes straight away. Under different circumstances, I would have never acted this way, but I simply knew that I could trust Charles. It did not seem that I had only known him for a short time. His soul felt incredibly familiar to me.

Even though we had very dissimilar upbringings—I attended schools in the United States and received a private education in Germany; while he was raised in American international schools in India and later attended English boarding school—we both shared a sense of seeking spirituality in the worldly wilderness and wanted to express our talents in creative pursuits, teaching and healing. I was very talented in languages, writing and healing whereas he was a musician who had studied yoga and pranayama since he was seven years old in India—a practice which successfully cured his asthma.

After we spent a month in the south of France together, Charles came to Germany to stay with me in my small studio flat near the anatomy department in the center of Cologne. He only brought a backpack with him when I came to collect him at the train station. Charles did not know a single word of German at the time. He ended up teaching English to professionals while I continued my medical studies at university. We spent Christmas 1999 with my parents near Frankfurt, in Germany and then travelled on to a Buddhist center in Berlin, where we planned to stay for a few days over New Year.

Because it was the Eve of the Year 2000, more than a million people had gathered on the streets of Berlin and there was a huge countdown in red letters beaming down at the crowds. Everybody pushed and shoved their way to the main event near the Brandenburg Tor; a concert which featured stars like Mike Oldfield. At midnight, the crowd went absolutely wild and I thought I was going deaf from the noise and the popping of champagne corks all around me. Finally, we managed to find a quieter corner and rang in the new millennium together. Suddenly, it did not matter anymore who else was there; the enormous crowds lost significance and I wandered off into the dark night with Charles.

That night we discussed many things and by the morning, I had agreed to marry him. Our first day as an engaged couple was 01/01/2000. I couldn't believe how much my life had changed since the last New Year's Eve, just a year ago, yet seemingly light authentic, when you realize who you really are, what you really want, and how to love yourself.

Realize Who You Are. That is the Second Step.

3. One of the gifts of the transitional process that we are experiencing on Earth right now is that humans are becoming aware of who they truly are: They are Souls, or Spiritual Entities, in human bodies; in other words, they can be Angels in human form.

Express Divine Love and become a Human Angel. That is the Third Step.

Meditation: Earth Angels

Sit in a comfortable position, either cross-legged on the floor or in a chair. Sit up tall with the spine straight, the shoulders relaxed and the chest open. Inhale the palms together and lightly press the knuckles of the thumbs into the sternum at the level of your heart (you should feel a little notch where the knuckles magically fit). Breathe slowly, smoothly and deeply into the belly and into the chest. Soften your gaze or lightly close the eyes. Let go of any thoughts or distractions and let the mind focus on feeling the breath move in and out of your body.

Once the mind feels quiet and still, bring your focus to the light pressure of the thumbs pressing against your chest and feeling the beating of the heart. Keep this focus for five minutes.

Now, gently release the hands and rub the palms together, making them very warm and energized. Place the right palm in the center of your chest and the left hand on top of the right. Close the eyes and feel the center of your chest warm and radiant, full of energy. See this energy as an emerald green light, radiating out from the center of your heart into the rest of your body. Feel this energy flowing out into the arms and hands, and flowing back into the heart. Stay with this visualization for five minutes.

Now that you feel completely saturated with heart chakra energy, gently release the palms and turn them outwards with the elbows bent, the shoulders relaxed and the chest open. Feel or visualize the green light love energy flowing out of your palms and into the world. You can direct it towards specific loved ones in your life or to all sentient beings.

To end your meditation, inhale the arms up towards the sky, connecting with the heavens, then exhale and lower the palms lightly to the floor, connecting with the earth. Take a moment or two to assimilate what you have experienced.

is a state of mind. Poverty focuses on lack, and abundance focuses on substance.

By realizing that we are made of Substance, we realize we are *always* connected to a constant, never ending stream of supply. This Substance that made us is the Substance of all the Universe, molded by Infinite Intelligence, or God. Universal Mind interpenetrates our mind and our mind interpenetrates and pervades our body. Its substance penetrates every atom of our body. We are never separate from it because *we are it.*

However, by focusing on lack and loss, we can hold ourselves separate from the flow of substance in our lives. You cannot create prosperity by thinking or talking about lack. Focusing on what you lack simply attracts more lack. Remember it is one of the principle Laws of Attraction that what we focus on grows. If we focus on what we lack, we simply attract more of the same. The good news is that abundance is always available to us because it is the nature of the Universe, and our own nature.

When we focus our thoughts and attention on the positive, such as expressing gratitude for the things we do have or see in our surroundings, then we attract more of what we want. In fact gratitude—acknowledgement of the Good in and around us—is one of the keys to achieving real prosperity.

The mighty oak tree starts as a small acorn. The seed in the earth never worries or frets or doubts that it will grow into a magnificent tree. It knows it purpose. It trusts and unfolds according to its nature.

The Bible advises us to trust and follow the example of nature; the results will be nothing short of miraculous: "Consider the lilies in the field, how they grow: they neither toil, nor spin; and yet I say to you that even Solomon in all his glory was not arrayed like one of these." (Matthew 6:27-29)

We can plant a small seed of a tree and see it expand and unfold into a magnificent demonstration. But if we doubt, lack trust, or lack faith, and we dig up our seed to check on its progress then we prevent its natural growth process and we are left with nothing. Then we might say: "See, it does not work. The tree does not grow." Not so. Our doubt, worry and anxiety have prevented it from growing. When given over to its own nature and the laws of the Universe, it grows perfectly.

So it is with ideas. We have a wonderful idea, we get excited about it, we set the wheels in motion—and then after a few days, when we do not see the progress, we exclaim, "It will never happen!" or "It does not work!" What has really happened is that the idea was unfolding perfectly into its own magnificent demonstration, but we have dug it up to check on its progress due to lack of faith and trust. You see how faith, conviction and trust are necessary ingredients in the manifestation process?

There is never a shortage of air, no matter how many people breathe. We are not taking away our neighbor's supply of air by breathing ourselves, just as we are not taking away someone else's supply of love, health, wealth, or success, by experiencing it ourselves. There is always enough for everyone. Universal Mind knows no lack; no limitation. There is much more money on the planet now than in any previous time in history that is known to us. There is no end to the supply; only so far as the finite mind perceives an end, or lack, or loss—then of course that is what it must experience.

By changing your thoughts, you can change your point of attraction, and the level of abundance that you experience in all areas of your life—relationships, career, health, wealth, joy, love —will change accordingly. This Law *always* works.

John R. Price refers to this unfailing universal principle when he writes, in *The Abundance Book*:

"And through the centuries, countless men and women accepted this truth, realized the law of infinite plenty within, and moved above the illusion of scarcity into the reality of unlimited wealth. They proved for themselves that the energy of abundance is constantly radiating from the Source within and flowing out to appear as money and financial well-being. (...) The secret is to be aware of this unfailing principle, to understand that lack is simply the outpicturing of false beliefs, and to know that as you make the correction in consciousness, you will become a channel for the activity of ever expanding affluence in your life."[27]

The following exercise will help you tune into your innate attraction and abundance.

Exercise: Prosperity Affirmations

Sit in a quiet, undisturbed place. Focus on your breathing. Do this for a few minutes until you feel you have connected with your heart chakra. Now affirm the following, while feeling the corresponding emotions strongly and visualizing yourself living the life of your dreams.

There are two steps to the manifestation process: wanting and believing. Thoughts with a lot of emotion behind them will manifest into your experience much faster—whether they are positive or negative. So, you may *want* your dream life very strongly, but not *believe* that you can have it so you do not expect it. This resistance manifests in your experience as the absence of your dream life. To manifest, you must both be clear about *what you want* and on the other side of the equation strongly *believe* that it is yours and fully *expect* it to enter your experience.

When you manifest an illness such as cancer, the wanting part of the equation is obviously very low but your belief in it is very strong and therefore it can manifest in your life experience.

To manifest therefore you have to equally *want* and *believe* or *expect*. These affirmations will program your mind to allow abundance into your life when you repeat them regularly with strong, positive emotion.

- *There is limitless supply and it belongs to me.*
- *I release the need for financial insecurity.*
- *I am financially secure.*
- *I am surrounded by loving, supportive, generous people.*
- *I release my need to feel needy and lackful.*
- *I release my fear of wealth, well-being and wholeness.*

- *I am healthy, wealthy and whole.*
- *I allow myself to prosper.*
- *I trust in my ability to create abundance.*
- *I have plenty in every area of my life.*
- *I open myself to receive the abundance of the Universe.*
- *I release my need for debt.*
- *I release my need for being poor.*
- *I can pay all my bills with ease.*
- *I am safe and secure.*
- *I enjoy a steady flow of positive energy.*
- *I am loved, accepted, acknowledged and appreciated.*
- *I have all the resources necessary to express myself authentically and creatively.*
- *I am living my dream.*
- *I am joyful, fulfilled, and successful.*
- *I AM Success!*
- *I AM Health!*
- *I AM Abundance!*

Bathe yourself in white healing light until every cell is illuminated by this awareness.

When you do this exercise regularly, you will notice a positive difference in your looks, your behaviour, your attraction, your manifestations, and your influence on others.

Money versus Spirituality?

There are people who say that you should not want money at all because the desire for money is materialistic and not spiritual. But you have to remember that you are at this moment here in this physical world, which is Spirit in materialized form. You are Spirit

Chapter 12

Healing and the Tao

People usually consider walking on water or in thin air a miracle.
But I think the real miracle is not to walk either on water or in thin air,
but to walk on earth.
Every day we are engaged in a miracle which we don't even recognize: a
blue sky, white clouds, green leaves,
the black, curious eyes of a child – our own two eyes.
All is a miracle.
- Thich Nhat Hanh

All Healing Comes From One Source

All life and all healing, which is a re-adjustment towards life, is, in essence, vibration. Ultimately, all healing comes from the one source. Whether the healing regime includes nutrition, exercise, medicine or even surgery, the aim is to bring about the consciousness of the forces within the body that aid in reproducing themselves – the awareness of creative, or God, forces.

The logic behind this is that whatever we see manifest in the material world is a reflection, or a shadow, of the real, or the spiritual, (soul) life. So, if you want to see the thoughts you have been thinking so far, just look at your life as it is right now.

All force, all life, is vibration because it all originates in one central vibration and its activity as it manifests in physicality, in form. This central or unitive vibration is a creative force which gives new beings, able to claim both their human and angelic inheritances, who will create the New Earth.

It is important to state, at this point, that it is imperative that those who make the transition into awareness of their angelic selves, be also aware of how important it is to be human and to be well grounded in the material dimensions or planes. The whole point of the Transition is to bring Heaven to Earth and manifest "paradise" right where you are – not to float away ungrounded with your "head in the clouds".

For Human Angels there is work to do: Creating a New Earth that will bring Heaven to Earth. And since "heaven" is not a place but a state of consciousness, these Human Angels must work to bring the higher dimensional states of consciousness to the Earth plane.

Once this is achieved, then a planetary culture will be birthed that will respect all beings as manifestations of the Divine Essence. And this culture will reflect that respect in its peace, harmony and creativity.

Meditation: How Can I Be Peace Right Now?

Choose a crystal and hold it in the palms of your hand. Feel its vibration. Get to know it.

Breathe gently. Make each breath out a little longer than the breath in. Look at your crystal; notice its color, pattern, shape. Hold your crystal in both hands, close your eyes and relax.

Now imagine you are inside your crystal. Let yourself move with the flow of the crystal. Let go of worldly thoughts and emotions and move deep into the centre of your crystal, imagine you are wandering through it exploring its inner beauty.

Sense the ancient wisdom held in every crystal cell around you. Be in this elevated state for a while, just soaking up the crystal's energy. Now, you are ready to ask the crystal for its specific message for you at this point in time.

Archangel Uriel, the "Flame of God", is head of the mighty angels of peace. Call to him and ask for his healing golden light to envelop you.

Ask: "What can I do to be Peace right now? How can I live Peace and be a shining example for those around me? How can I embody Peace right now? What is my unique way to spread the light of Peace to my fellow beings right now?"

When you are ready, slowly allow yourself to come back to physical reality. Say three times:

"Archangel Uriel and angels of peace, I accept the gift of peace. In my body, in my mind, in my heart, in my soul."

Put your crystal aside and ground yourself by imagining roots coming from your feet and going down into the ground. Move your toes, shake your hands and just sit for a moment reflecting on what you saw and how you felt. Note down any messages you received.

This is what true healing is really all about; a holistic approach that heals the heart, synthesizes many valid paths or soul journeys into one personal path to Wholeness, Wellness, and Wonderment. Everybody is on the same journey through various steps, or dimensions, of consciousness. It may appear that decay, deprivation and regression is prevalent around you, but they are human fabrications and can be undone by the human mind as well.

The fastest way to do this is to be kind to yourself and others; to be an example of peace right where you stand. Tune into your Divine Inheritance, become a Human Angel and display the full potential of the human soul.

Everybody who is human is here for a reason. Everybody is on a journey; a personal journey of consciousness which will bring them back home; a place where ecstasy, joy, creativity, abundance and the dance of life is the natural state of being.

Apostle John's Inner Journey

We find the perfect illustration for the soul's journey told by the Apostle John during his exile on the Greek island of Patmos in the Book of Revelation. The visions, experiences, names, churches, places, dragons, and cities are all symbolic of the internal struggles that manifest for the individual as consciousness as soul development unfolds and the personal vibration is raised to a higher level. Every soul, or divine thought, begins at a vibrational starting point and goes through incarnations, or lifetimes, to learn its (vibrational) lessons. There are no shortcuts in the divine plan.

We are not "doing it wrong" when we encounter obstacles or undesired manifestations, such as illness. We are, by our very Beingness, always God's children; or outflowings of the one source, the divine vibration. Suffering, illness and lack, when it is experienced, doubtlessly feels real to us and we have the corresponding emotions of dislike, sadness, pain and fear. However, we can always build on the vibration in which we are at the moment.

Every vantage point is an opportunity to expand and grow. By knowing what you do not want, you simultaneously know what you do want. If you do not want illness, pain and suffering, you know that you do want health, joy and freedom. Every time this "negative" (lack of health, lack of money, etc.) experience occurs, your focus gets stronger and stronger. Whatever you focus on, manifests as your experience.

You have been given free will. The ultimate power lies within you.

Vibrational Healing

Nelson Mandela, the great South African abolitionist and philosopher, referred to this potential within every soul when he said:

"Our deepest fear is not that we are inadequate. Our deepest fear is that we are powerful beyond measure. It is our light, not our darkness, that frightens us most. We ask ourselves, 'Who am I to be brilliant, gorgeous, talented, and famous?' Actually, who are you not to be? You are a child of God. Your playing small does not serve the world. There is nothing enlightened about shrinking so that people won't feel insecure around you. We were born to make manifest the glory of God that is within us. It's not just in some of us; it's in all of us. And when we let our own light shine, we unconsciously give other people permission to do the same. As we are liberated from our own fear, our presence automatically liberates others."

The Tao knows only one stream—the stream of well-being. It does not emanate two streams, one of goodness and one of badness, or one of wellness and one of illness. Your soul-essence is goodness –health, wellness, happiness, success and wealth.

Exercise: Being in the Stream of the Tao

Carl Jung said: "Who looks outside, dreams; who looks inside, awakes."

You come with an in-built navigation system: Your emotions. They will always tell you exactly how you are placed concerning the stream of Well-Being that eternally runs through you. Are you —mentally—holding yourself apart from it? The questions to ask yourself are:

Right now, am I in this stream?

Am I permitting it to flow through me?

Am I consenting to feeling happy, healthy, successful, loveable and wealthy?

Am I allowing the experience of goodness in my life?

Right now—am I experiencing happiness?

Do I feel wonderment at everything around me?

Am I open to the miracle of life that constantly unfolds before my eyes?"

Your thoughts are free. Think in ways that make you happy.

Chapter 13

Nourishing the Body Temple

Nourished with a sense of the Unity, you will be able to digest the differences.
- N. Sri Ram

Spiritual Nutrition

Water is Life. We know that we cannot live for long without water. Even our food is mostly water; and our drink even more so. There is probably nothing in our life that forms as much a part of our daily routine as eating and drinking. The French author François de La Rochefoucauld (1613-1680) wrote: "To eat is a necessity, but to eat intelligently is an art."

Many of us make our food choices unconsciously. Often, while in the supermarket, we just grab what is available at the time, or what seems to suit our budget and keeps the shelf and stomach full. Shopping for food is a routine task so we often take it for granted and as something to "get done" and "get over with" so that we can move on to more interesting pastimes. But we have to understand that what we buy will eventually end up in our mouths and bodies. In this way, the initial choice is made while piling food into our cart and then paying for it and taking it home.

It is wonderful that there is so much food, to suit all budgets, tastes and diets, so readily available to us in the Western world. We are grateful to the suppliers who work very hard and have made it their life's aim to provide us with food, drink and nourishment.

we are. This affects all aspects of ourselves, including our spirituality. As nutrition experts teach, health is not found in isolated nutrients and supplements, but in a broad and varied plant-based diet. Incorporating vegetables and fruits of every color in the rainbow is an easy way to ensure that we are getting all the nutrients we need.

2. When we eat for physical, emotional and spiritual health, our whole being soars. When we eat for emotional reasons, eat too fast, or eat when we're angry, bored or sad, we tend to feel guilty, depressed and bad about ourselves, the opposite of what food really symbolizes—the giving and enhancement of vibrant life. Unfortunately, emotional eating tends to become a pattern and we become trapped in poor eating habits.

3. With over 65% of Americans either overweight or obese and health care costs higher than anywhere else, it's plain to see that the United States have challenges to overcome in health education and care. Hyperthyroidism, diabetes, asthma, and coronary artery disease are major health problems in the U.S. and these diseases are often linked to poor diets, particularly those which include significant amounts of highly processed foods, refined sugar and wheat. While many of us would acknowledge that great emotional and spiritual growth can be achieved through suffering, most people will not deliberately choose this route to personal growth. What we need therefore, is clear scientific information on how to be healthy. For those of us who may not be able to afford expensive and exotic foods, rest assured that these healthy foods are not simply the healthiest but are often also the most accessible and affordable choices.

4. Looking at indigenous societies that still practice traditional ways of eating and comparing them to developed countries such as the United States and the United Kingdom, we see not only that eating habits and disease prevalence can be extremely different, but also the spiritual reverence for life. For instance, indigenous communities in the Amazon eat a primarily plant-based diet and do not experience the "affluent" diseases we experience in the U.S. and U.K. Many of these same communities are extraordinarily respectful of their environment—often having songs and stories about each plant, and giving thanks for every animal that helps them live and thrive. These people dance, sing, and vibrate joy in a way that is quite unusual in modern societies. This is an expression of gratitude, respect and spirituality.

5. As our phones constantly ring, our inbox overflows with emails and our neck and shoulders coil in pain, we feel continuously reminded of the need to produce, rush, and work. What we need most is the time and the ease to enjoy life. When you eat for health and spirituality, in other words, when you nourish the Body Temple, you make one of the absolutely most essential acts in life—eating—not only healthy and enjoyable, but also easy.

Nothing in this universe is alone or separate. Everything is connected. Only the human mind creates divisions and separations. So while we allow our Higher Self to shine forth, why not give that joyous dancing Self a supporting hand by making healthy food choices?

mood and sleep patterns than the quick fixes, side effects and possible hazards of drugs and nutrient supplementation. The angels give guidance that will increase the flow and regulation of your serotonin. When they ask you to eat vibrant foods, to connect with nature, and to exercise—they are not trying to spoil your fun. These are easy and enjoyable ways to naturally improve your mood and energy levels.

Rich food sources of tryptophan – serotonin[28] include:

- Sea vegetables, blue-green algae
- Fish
- Sea food
- Tofu, Soy Milk, Soy Yoghurt and Soy Beans
- Brown rice
- Chocolate (over 75%)
- Oats
- Bananas
- Dates
- Figs
- Milk (fat content at least 3.5%; raw milk is best if mostly unavailable nowadays)
- Cottage cheese (and all fermented dairy products such as buttermilk, German quark, kefir, yoghurt, etc.)
- Turkey
- Almonds
- Peanuts and peanut butter
- Legumes

Sea vegetables, shrimp, sea food and fish contain the highest levels of tryptophan.

The levels of tryptophan in some common foods are:

- Algae, fish and other sea foods 800-1,300 mg/lb
- Meats 1,000-1,300 mg/lb
- Poultry 600-1,200 mg/lb
- Peanuts, roasted with skin 800 mg/cup
- Sesame seeds 700 mg/cup
- Dry, whole lentils 450 mg/ cup
- Cottage cheese 450mg/cup

The high fibre content of sea vegetables makes you feel full sooner and thus prevents overeating, dissolves excess fat, and has a slightly laxative effect, thus assisting passage through the intestines. The University of Madrid has concluded that sea vegetables are a food "rich in proteins, minerals, vitamins and other specific nutrients, such as polyunsaturated fatty acids [which is] noteworthy for its high content in minerals and trace elements. All the elements needed by the human body are found in sufficient quantities in algae."[30]

Storage

For most people, sea vegetables are available only in dried form. In unopened packages, dried sea vegetables will keep for a long time, at least until the expiration date shown on the plastic wrapper. Once you have opened the package, keep the sea weed or the flakes in an air-tight container stored in a cool place. If the sea vegetables absorb moisture and become soggy, they can be dried on a sheet in the oven set at a low temperature (120-140F or 50-60C) for about 1 hour.

Green Tea

Archangel Raphael says that Green Tea is green in color because it has extraordinary healing qualities. This tea is medicine in its purest form but you do have to show it the reference and respect it deserves.

The secret of Green Tea lies in the fact it is rich in catechin polyphenols, particularly epigallocatechin gallate (EGCG). EGCG is a powerful anti-oxidant; besides inhibiting the growth of cancer cells, it kills already existing cancer cells without harming healthy tissue. It also has a beneficial effect in lowering LDL ("bad") cholesterol levels, and inhibiting the abnormal formation of blood clots. The latter takes on added importance when you consider that thrombosis (the formation of abnormal blood clots) is the primary cause of heart attacks and stroke.

Green Tea also gives us an additional key to finding the reasoning behind the "French Paradox". For years, researchers were puzzled by the fact that, despite consuming a diet rich in fat, French people have a lower incidence of heart disease than Americans. Red wine, which is drunk as an accompaniment to meals in France, contains resveratrol, a polyphenol that limits the detrimental effects of smoking and a fatty diet. In a 1997 study, researchers from the University of Kansas determined that EGCG (found in Green Tea) is twice as powerful as resveratrol, which helps to explain why the rate of heart disease among Japanese men is fairly low, even though approximately seventy-five percent are smokers.

Why don't other teas have similar health-giving properties? Green, oolong, and black teas are all derived from the leaves of the *Camellia sinensis* plant. What differentiates Green Tea is the way it is processed. Green tea leaves are steamed, which prevents the EGCG compound from being oxidized. By contrast, black and oolong tea leaves are made from fermented leaves, which results in the EGCG being converted into other compounds which are not nearly as effective in preventing and fighting various diseases.

Green Tea can help dieters and those looking for a nutritious, healthy way to shed excess fat. A study at the University of Geneva in Switzerland showed that men who were given a combination of caffeine and green tea extract burned more calories than those given only caffeine or a placebo.

Green Tea can also help prevent tooth decay. Just as its bacteria-destroying abilities can help prevent food poisoning, it can also kill the bacteria that cause dental plaque.

Historically, tea consumption had its origin in China more than 4000 years ago. Green Tea has been used as both a beverage and a method of traditional systems of medicine in most of Asia, including China, Japan, Taiwan, Vietnam, Korea, India and Thailand, to assist with ailment and diseases ranging from controlling bleeding and helping heal wounds to regulating body temperature, blood sugar and promoting digestion.

The *Kissa Yojoki* (Tea and Health Care) from 1191, written by Japanese Zen priest Eisai (1141-1215), describes how drinking Green Tea can have a positive effect on the five vital organs, especially the heart. The book discusses the medicinal qualities of tea, which include diminishing the effects of alcohol, acting as a stimulant, curing blotchiness, quenching thirst, eliminating indigestion, curing beriberi disease, preventing fatigue, and improving urinary and brain function.[31]

If you want to partake of the remarkable health benefits of Green Tea, it is important not to buy the cheap and second-rate versions of this marvelous gift of nature because the cheaper *Sencha* kinds that are widely available in supermarkets and Asia stores are not very potent.

Gyokuro Asahi is the rarest Japanese tea of all, being grown under special bamboo shades to give a tea with a uniquely fragrant flavor. The name *Gyokuro* refers to the pale green color of the infusion. This Green Tea has traditionally been served to emperors, luminaries, and revered guests as a special honor. The fine emerald needle-shaped leaves result in a bright, aromatic, exquisite tea that takes its time to brew and savor.

There are many guidelines to brewing Gyokuro and most advise a short immersion time of 1-3 minutes to preserve the light, delicate flavor. Medical studies have shown that this short time period does not allow for sufficient extraction of polyphenols, specifically EGCG.[32]

The proper way of brewing a cup of Gyokuro Green Tea for maximum benefits and flavor is this:

rays of light. Surrounding it is your causal body—glorious rainbow-colored spheres composed of the primordial bequest of light rays or frequencies to your soul. Each vibratory color represents a specific virtue which you have developed through different incarnations by your positive thoughts, words and actions. Positivity is nothing else than being in alignment with your true, or spiritual, nature.

Your true self always feels happy. Your true nature is the cosmic stream of continuous well-being. When you do not think at all; that is, do not create thoughts that negate (or turn away from) the stream, you feel happy, light and present. *You feel Yourself.*

The blessed Mother Mary performed this illustrious service on behalf of her son, Jesus, who, through her nurturing love and devotion, was able to fulfill his mission of fully manifesting the Christ ideal as an example for all humans to follow. After Mother Mary's ascension, she appeared to Saint Bernadette Soubirous and informed the young girl: "I am the Immaculate Conception." On earth, she embodies holding the immaculate concept with constancy for all of God's children. In this way, Mary shows us what is possible and is the prime example for us all to emulate.

Holding the Immaculate Concept for The Self

It is imperative that we first hold the immaculate concept for ourselves by attuning to our own Higher Self and maintaining a perception of oneness through presence and awareness of our own divine nature. Once we have learned to live in this unified field of stillness and beingness and maintain our spiritual presence, even when confronted with challenges and obstacles in our life, we can extend the science of the immaculate concept to all those around us with greater ease and knowledge.

Every Person is Already Whole

One key in mastering this science, given to us by the Ascended Masters, is to behold every person in consciousness as a newborn infant or soul, without guile or blemish, pure and whole and wholly dependent upon his divine Parent. Even amidst the temporary playing out of personal problems in karmic situations, we can help each individual in overcoming their karmic patterns by seeing with the eyes of unconditional love, sending them positive and healing thoughts and understanding that everyone who is in a human body has their work cut out. Being human is never easy, even if you are enlightened, you are still in a physical shell and housed by a human body which is fragile, temporary and focused in time and space.

By not judging others or condemning them based on our subjective view of a minuscule part of their life and soul journey, we can amplify hope and emanate a field of belief based on certainty and knowing that they can be happy, successful and fulfill God's plan.

In Golden Age civilizations of the future, the science of the immaculate concept will be taught and practiced by all from early childhood onward just as it was practiced in Golden Ages of the past. This spiritual science is a key in manifesting the longevity of all divine cultures and is what allows every Ascended Master to maintain his or her own immortality in God's Spirit.

The Maha Chohan of the Eighth Ray

The Maha Chohan is the representative of the Holy Spirit for earth. His name means "great Lord" or "Great Master". *Maha* means great in Sanskrit; as in Mahatma, which translates to "Great Soul". He is also the chohan of the eighth ray, which synthesizes all of the seven rays into pure white light. The Maha Chohan carries the golden pink flame of God's love and comfort. This quality is exemplified in the wings of the angels, the divine messengers, which enfold us, comfort us and hold us unconditionally. His retreat is over the island of Sri Lanka, where he oversees and directs the activities of the seven chohans of the rays, who serve willingly under him. As the chohan of the eighth ray, he expands the sacred flame of each of the seven rays which combine into the pure white light of the Holy Spirit. This golden pink light ray balances the energies of Christ—the divine spark in our hearts—with the energies of

201

the Holy Spirit (the Tao, or the Divine Matrix that underlies and "breathes" or "births" all life).

As the representative of the Holy Spirit, the Maha Chohan works with the seven chohans to prepare students on the spiritual path to become ready to receive the nine gifts of the Holy Spirit, enumerated as: "For to one is given by the Spirit the word of wisdom; to another the word of knowledge by the same Spirit; To another faith by the same Spirit; to another the gifts of healing by the same Spirit; To another the working of miracles; to another prophecy; to another discerning of spirits; to another diverse kinds of tongues; to another the interpretation of tongues: But all these worketh that one and the selfsame Spirit, dividing to every man severally as he will."[34] The nine gifts of the Holy Spirit can be broken down into three categories, namely Revelation Gifts (Word of Wisdom, Word of Knowledge and Discerning of Spirits), Power Gifts (Faith, Healings and Miracles), and Inspiration Gifts (Prophecy, Diverse Tongues, Interpretation of Tongues).

The Maha Chohan was embodied as the blind Greek poet Homer who wrote the epics the *Iliad* and the *Odyssey*. In his final embodiment, he was a shepherd in India and the spiritual light he quietly emanated and spread while tending his sheep effected the spiritual progression of millions of souls.

The Maha Chohan and his pink flame angels bring love, joy and comfort to all life. They work closely with the forces of nature, from the largest ocean to the smallest drop of water and even down below the level of atomic particles. They infuse every molecule of oxygen with the sacred breath, or fire of the Holy Spirit. The Maha Chohan ignites the threefold flame at the heart thereby fusing the breath (or life force, or spirit) of God with the physical body when a child takes its first breath. He is also present at the time of transition when a person expends their last breath of air, and the flame of life is withdrawn from the "earthly shell".

The Holy Spirit of God, or the life force provided by Tao to all individualized manifestations, whether here on earth or in our galaxy or in the cosmos is perfectly described by Paul:

"When you sow, you do not plant the body that will be, but just a seed, perhaps of wheat or of something else. But God gives it a body as he has determined, and to each kind of seed he gives its own body. All flesh is not the same: Men have one kind of flesh, animals have another, birds another and fish another. There are also heavenly bodies and there are earthly bodies; but the splendor of the heavenly bodies is one kind, and the splendor of the earthly bodies is another. The sun has one kind of splendor, the moon another and the stars another; and star differs from star in splendor."[35]

You can consciously invoke the presence of the Maha Chohan by inviting him into your secret chamber in the heart: "This body and this heart are a vessel for the Holy Spirit. Holy Spirit, I invite you and welcome you. My secret chalice is filled. I am enlightened by the divine flame. I am infused with divine love. Every cell in my body is filled with the light of the Holy Spirit. I AM divine love in action NOW."

The Threefold Flame in the Heart

The Mermaids rule emotions and emotions are born in the heart.

The God–Flame Within

It all begins in the heart. The heart is the repository for the flame of God. "God has poured out his love into our hearts by the Holy Spirit, whom he has given us."[36] This flame is the essence of God, blazing within our physical form. Called the "threefold flame" it can only be seen at higher frequencies. It is real and exists, but, in the same way you need a radio to pick up radio waves or a telephone to hear faraway voice frequencies, this flame can only be "received" by senses with adequately attuned receptors. The threefold flame sustains our physical life and represents the sacred trinity of love, wisdom and power. It is placed in our hearts at birth and is withdrawn at transition.

Transformations of the Threefold Flame:
The Resurrection and Ascension Flames and Spirals

I have spoken to many people who have confirmed to me that they can physically feel the Divine flame in their hearts after undergoing certain steps of soul development. I have also come to experience this Flame personally and I can feel and see it clearly in meditation. It is most often described as a feeling of warmth, or a glowing or even burning sensation at the level of the heart.

I experience it as an outflowing, or a beaming of opalescent white light—so bright that it is luminous and seems to belong to a higher dimension—originating in the heart center and filling every cell of my body until I am not physically present anymore (to my awareness) but find myself in a space of pure intelligence, or pure consciousness. This pure white light "illumination" extends from me in all directions; blessing, uplifting and benefitting all it touches.

The most important aspect of the Divine Flame, whether you can feel it or not, is its transformative quality as expressed in your life when your focus and intention to live your life's plan, which is the same as God's plan for your soul, strengthens and grows. God's plan is contained within the Divine spark, the threefold Flame at your heart; so you are always carrying it with you. By focusing on your life's purpose you are also focusing on God's plan for you; because the two are one and the same. When you strengthen your resolve to live life to the fullest, and to the highest good, you set the wheels in motion to grow and expand the three plumes seated at your heart center.

This Flame is your personal "Fountain of Youth". Once the plumes become balanced, a miraculous action begins to take place— the plumes begin to spin and swirl around each other, emanating mother-of-pearl colored radiant light. The Flame is transformed, even as we are being transformed, and is now called the "resurrection flame". Through our dedication to the God-flame within, as expressed in our life's purpose, we have fanned the Divine spark, the threefold Flame, into a swirling action, forming an energy spiral or vortex, igniting our awareness of the soul's immortality. Ultimately, devotion to this spiraling resurrection flame magnetizes a force field around us termed the "resurrection spiral". This action of light vibrations is evidence that we are heading towards ascension. The next step of evolution comes when we hold the immaculate concept constantly in our consciousness for all people and all things. As a result of our single-pointed focus, the resurrection flame accelerates its motion and spirals even faster. The mother-of-pearl emanation becomes brilliant, dazzling and sparkling pure white. It is now the flame of the ascension, magnetizing around us the "ascension spiral"; or energy current or vortex. The Divine spark of God has become a Divine Fire, and an ascension vehicle that lifts us upwards to the Space of our Presence.

It all begins in the heart. It begins in the secret place where God dwells within the flame, the place from which our physical heart beats in synch with cosmic symphonies, the place that pulses and forms the rhythm of the inbreath and outbreath of the Holy Spirit, the place that sets in motion the flow of our life's blood through the circulatory system to animate our organs and give life to our form.

Within the heart, inside a secret chamber, resides the threefold flame—where Heaven and Earth meet.

with your emotions and you will experience situations and people on the basis of feeling, primarily.

The four Zodiac Elements—Fire, Earth, Air and Water—are also known as the Triplicities since there are three signs belonging to each Elemental category. This trio of signs shares a character pattern; and certain inclinations, personality traits and modes of experiencing and processing the world.

The Elements are also known as the Four Humors in Greek philosophy. In the fifth century, the Greek philosopher Empedocles originated the terms "Fire", "Earth", "Air" and "Water" explaining the nature of the universe as an interaction of two opposing principles he termed "Love" and "Conflict" which manipulated, influenced and controlled the four Elements. Empedocles also stated that these four Elements were all equal and came into being at the same time, each ruling its own domain and each possessing its own individual character. He speculated that distinctive mixtures of the four Elements produced the different natures of things.

The fifth element, Spirit, is referred to as "Quinta Essentia", or Akasha. It is present in all elements and things. Akasha is the life force—the basic substance of the Universe and the soul or spiritual essence of an individual. It is the subtle spiritual substance that pervades all space; not ether (although it has sometimes been mixed up with this) but an etheric, intelligent and self-aware substance of a spiritual rather than material nature which, in ancient writings, is said to operate by means of sound, or vibration.

"In the beginning was the Word, and the Word was with God." (John 1:1) The basic sound, or vibration of the universe is OM. Essentially, Akasha stands apart from the Four Elements of the Zodiac and is not depicted within an individual's horoscope because it transcends and enlivens (is present in) all the other elements. Akasha points to the freedom of humankind and embodies the "mystery of the eternal".

Water is the ruler of the Fourth (Cancer; Moon; Home, Nurture, Past), Eighth (Scorpio; Pluto; Death, Re-Birth and Transformation) and Twelfth (Pisces; Neptune; Spirit, Surrender, Secrets) Houses of the Zodiac.

Water is Love

Water, like the Mermaids, is linked to emotions and the subconscious. Strong, enduring and essential to life on this planet, water is associated with love, emotion, purification, cleansing, healing, compassion, intuition, clairsentience (clear feeling), psychic abilities, relationships, family and the secrets and mysteries of the Self and the Cosmos.

Physically, all life on Earth is dependent on water; and water is symbolic of the universal womb, the Cosmic Mother, birth and fertility; or the sustaining and giving of life.

This Element is equally life-giving and life-destroying; it can manifest as a peaceful tropical lagoon or as a fierce destructive tsunami, it can flow wherever it is needed and where it can't even be seen, it is fluid and changeable, it can be gentle and soft or hard and crashing, it can escape and withdraw, and it can be used to cleanse and purify in both a physical and a spiritual sense.

Water is able to adopt many forms; it is changeable, adaptive and transformative—it can be liquid or gaseous (steam) or frozen (ice).

This Element and the Mermaids remember the past and foresee the future. Mermaids correspond to the emotional body of the human nature. Humans—and especially those born under a water sign—are as changeable, subtle and able to flow and integrate in secret places as is water itself.

Mermaids and those with a strong emphasis on the water element in the birth chart can sense moods, tap into the atmosphere of an environment and read minds—then act accordingly. Their approach to life is emotion-led, this means that experience is processed via the emotional body and on the basis of feelings and then evaluated and expressed by the emotional correspondences of these feelings. These individuals are sometimes difficult to figure out for others as they can change at the drop of a hat, have an uncanny ability to "know" what the other is feeling and can sometimes almost seem to merge with their opposite which can be unsettling for those used to boundaries, order and definition. They are also like clams—if they feel unappreciated or "unseen", they will retreat into their shell and lock everybody out.

which speak to us about the nature of the Mermaids and the water elementals. It can also help us to understand ourselves and Mother Earth better, because humans and the surface of the planet both contain 70% water.

- **Aspect/ Polarity:** Feminine. This pole can also be named as Yin, or Anima (after C. G. Jung). This is not a reference to gender but to the associated type of energy. The feminine aspect rules the right brain (the nerve strands cross over at the neck so the right brain rules the left side of the body). This energy is receptive and conceived as being less active and focused in the material world, which adds sensitivity, intuition, and emotional and spiritual depth to the character. Yin, or Female signs are described as negative; like a battery has two poles: positive and negative.

  Negative Signs tend toward introversion and choose to draw upon personal resources rather than seek out external stimuli. Such individuals are naturally more intuitive, sensitive and nurturing than are the Zodiac Signs of Positive, masculine polarity (Aries, Gemini, Leo, Libra, Sagittarius and Aquarius).

  However, on the flip side, Negative Signs are also prone to show more caution, shyness and reserve than their Positive counterparts, with a tendency to keep personal feelings (experienced intensely) under a close lid. Taurus is the most introverted of the Negative Signs (with Virgo a close second). Feminine signs (Taurus, Cancer, Virgo, Scorpio, Capricorn and Pisces) are nocturnal, or night-oriented by nature.

  The Yin polarity of the Tao is depicted as black; and associated with the night, the moon, and the secrets and mystery of the cosmos.

  All Zodiac Signs governed by the Elements of Fire and Air are considered to be Masculine in nature. Thus,

Libra (ruled by air) is considered Masculine (as are Aries, Gemini, Leo, Sagittarius and Aquarius).

Masculine signs are traditionally conceived as being more active and less receptive than their Feminine counterparts, which are ruled by the Elements of Earth and Water (the Zodiac Signs of Taurus, Cancer, Virgo, Scorpio, Capricorn and Pisces).

Masculine signs focus primarily on intelligence and activity; both in the physical sense and the mental sense. Masculine signs are said to be diurnal or day-oriented. The Yang polarity of the Tao is depicted as white; and associated with the day, the sun, and intellectual and physical activity.

- **Angel of Water**: Gabriel, Archangel of the West.

- **Season**: Autumn, the time of lack of moisture on earth and indicative of impending snow.

- **Virtue**: Benevolence. This element represents charity, compassion, kindness, service, generosity, goodwill. Water is interested in the welfare of others. By nature, it is philanthropic. Water feels very deeply, it "soaks vibrations up like a sponge" so it can harbor resentment for uncleared misalignments and deeds but its fundamental joy comes from helping others and being of service.

- **Core/ Individuality**: Service. Water embodies co-operation, tolerance and hospitality. Water is sociable and truly humanitarian. The core or individuality, the essence, of the water element is described as "service" because of its unselfishness and heart-felt devotion to the welfare of humanity. Water will unconditionally come to the aid of the sick, the deprived, the defective, and the unfortunate, whether the individual in question things build inwardly. When this happens, water can be incredibly destructive, like a pressure valve.

When this pressure is directed inwardly, against the self, as it often is with introvert (Negative, Yin) individuals, the result can be eating disorders, alcoholism, co-dependency, gambling, or any other form of addiction and compulsive behavior.

The challenge for water, and Yin, patterns of behaviour is the balance of caring for others with caring of the self. Water elementals are poled, and extremely adept, at caring for others. They have to learn to extend the unconditional love, tolerance and acceptance to their own selves as well.

- **Humor**: In ancient Greek medicine, each of the four humors became associated with an element. The four humors of Hippocratic medicine were black bile (*melancholia*), yellow bile (*cholera*), phlegm (*phlegma*), and blood (*sanguis*). Water was identified with phlegm, since both were cold, wet and moist. In ancient and medieval medicine, water and phlegm are associated with the season of winter, since it increases the qualities of cold and moisture; the feminine; the brain; and the western point of the compass.

- **Vedic Philosophy**: The element of water is associated with Chandra (the Moon), and Shukra (Venus). These planetary bodies represent feelings, love, intuition and imagination.

- **Colors**: Green, Blue, Blue-Green, Turquoise, Grey, Black and Indigo.

- **Sacred Geometry**: In the *Timaeus*, Plato's major cosmological dialogue, the Platonic solid associated with water is the icosahedron which is formed from twenty equilateral triangles. This makes water the element with the greatest number of sides, which Plato regarded as appropriate because water flows out of one's hand when picked up, as if it is constituted of many tiny balls.[40]

- **Moon Phase**: Third Quarter

- **Positive Characteristics**: Sensitivity, Compassion, Courage, Intuition, Charity and Grace.

- **Negative Characteristics**: Self-Destruction, Insecurity and Self-Doubt.

- **Sense**: Taste.

- **Symbols**: Shells, Chalice, Cauldron, Mirrors, Goblets and Cups of Water.

- **Musical Instruments**: Conch Shells, Cymbals, Bells and all Instruments made of Resonant Metals.

- **Plants and Trees**: Water Plants such as Lotus, Lily Pads, Reeds, Algae, Herbs, Ferns, Mosses, Rushes, Sea Weeds, Water Lilies, and the Willow Tree.

- **Stones:** Larimar, Aquamarine, Pearl, Moonstone, Lapis Lazuli, Blue Sapphire, Blue Topaz, Jade, Agate, Amethyst, and River Pebbles.

- **Metals:** Mercury, Silver and Copper.

- **Locations:** Water is present in most places on Earth but it is most dominant in places that are moist, wet, steamy, humid, liquid, fluid, or icy. Lakes, Springs, Streams, Rivers, Beaches, Oceans, Wells, Fountains, Rainforests, Swamps, Marshes, Swimming Pools, Bathtubs, Showers, Health Spas, Steam Rooms. Water is also the element of intuition, dreams, and "the dark side of the moon" (cosmic secrets) so it is prevalent in bedrooms.

- **Direction**: West. This direction is identified with the non-physical realms because the Sun is seen to set (leave materially) in the West. In numerous European legends, the Realms of the Dead are separated from the Realm of the Living by a body of water, such as a river or explain the color purple to someone who has never seen it, or describe the taste of an orange to someone who has never eaten one, you cannot sufficiently and satisfactorily describe the inner truth to someone who has not experienced it. To connect with this truth that "surpasses all understanding" (referring to the fact that it cannot be grasped by the left-brained intellectual way of thinking) and have a direct experience of it, which instantaneously transforms all doubt, skepticism, and uncertainty, there is only one route: To go within.

How do we find the Truth that is locked within?

In meditation, we can learn how to transform our mind from negative to positive, from disturbed to peaceful, from unhappy to happy. Overcoming negative mental states and cultivating constructive thoughts is the purpose of meditation.

The Mermaids know that meditation will transform us. This is a profound spiritual practice you can enjoy throughout the day, not just while sitting still in meditation.

Instructions on how to meditate abound. In fact, a quick look in the event section of most daily newspapers shows that there is a confusing array of meditation schools and esoteric traditions offering courses, seminars and retreats aimed at teaching interested Westerners how to meditate. Once the initial bafflement is overcome and the often foreign terms and rituals have been successfully decoded it soon becomes obvious, however, that most schools in fact teach one (or a combination) of three main meditation techniques, namely mindfulness meditation, concentrative meditation, or analytical meditation.

Mindfulness Meditation

Mindfulness meditation involves paying attention to the processes of the mind in order to become aware of the continuous flow of sensations and feelings, images, thoughts, sounds, smells, and other mental activity. The trick here is to be aware of the mental processes as they occur without becoming involved in them. The meditator sits quietly and simply witnesses whatever thoughts come up. He or she does not react to or identify with any thoughts, memories, worries, or images that arise in the mind. This practice is used to cultivate a peaceful, clear, and non-reactive state of mind. Mindfulness meditation can be likened to a wide-angle lens. The meditator is focused in the present and aware of all mental activity as it takes place without becoming involved in it.

Concentrative Meditation

Concentrative meditation may be likened to the zoom lens of a camera. Here, the meditator purposefully narrows down her field of attention and a single object becomes the focus of awareness. The chosen object of meditation may be the breath, an image, or a sound (mantra). Single-minded concentration on the object of meditation to the exclusion of all other thoughts stills the mind, and allows greater awareness and clarity to emerge. The simplest form of concentrative meditation is to sit quietly, focusing the attention on the breath.

Yogic philosophy teaches that there is a direct correlation between our breath and our state of mind. When we are anxious, scared, upset, or distracted, our breath follows suit by becoming shallow, agitated, and irregular. When we are calm, focused, and composed on the other hand, we find that our breath is equally relaxed—slow, deep, and regular. The ongoing continuous rhythm of inhalation and exhalation provides a natural object of meditation.

By focusing the awareness on the breath, the mind eventually becomes absorbed in the rhythm of inhalation and exhalation. As a result, the breath becomes slow and deep, and the mind more tranquil and receptive.

Breathing Meditation

Breathing meditation is usually taught as a preliminary stage of meditation. Nevertheless, it is a very worthwhile practice with quite powerful effects. Breathing meditation is easy to do and it shows techniques and achieving lucid dreams, which is really just constant awareness, even in altered, or heightened, stages of perception, you will improve and transform your waking life as well. You will cease to be restricted by automatic reactions (which come from the unconscious mind) and be more in control of your experience. By realizing that you can influence your dreams with your mind, that they are actually products of your mind, you will recognize the extent to which you are in control of your waking life as well. It may not seem so at first, but every entity, or soul, manifests their own life experiences. If we are always creating, and our entire life is a reflection of our thoughts, then we may as well create a life we love. This is what the Mermaids want us to do and why they teach lucid dreaming techniques.

These methods are a "quick path" to awareness at different levels of consciousness and recognizing the Power of the Mind.

Mermaid Exercise:

4 Easy Steps to lucid dreaming

Step 1: You are not subject to any physical laws in your dreams. You have complete freedom. Instead of walking, you can fly. While you are sailing through the skies you may spontaneously decide that you would like to explore the unfathomable depths of the ocean without the need for special equipment for breathing, or travel at lightning speed and investigate the infinite cosmos and myriads of planets and stars without a ship to encapsulate you. You can be a mermaid with a beautiful fish tail the scales on which shimmer in all the colors of the rainbow. You can experience the luxurious silky smoothness of tropical waters on your skin and the abundance of sea life around you.

There are no limits to what you can be or do. As soon as the thought is in your mind, it is translated into your reality. You perceive and experience exactly what is in your mind; as if the universe takes a snap shot of your thoughts and develops them exactly as you pictured them.

It will likely take a while for you to fully appreciate the idea that you can do whatever you imagine—you'll likely hold on to the belief that some things are just not possible during your first attempts at lucid dreaming. Of course, as you believe, so it is done unto you—so as long as you believe something is impossible, it will be.

Alice in Wonderland says: "I believe in six impossible things before breakfast."

That is the Spirit of inventors, of progress and of creativity. It is the Spirit of God.

Step 2: Lucid dreams are usually induced by certain cues or signs—you need to be conscious enough to acknowledge these signs if you wish to advance your awareness in the dream world. Settle on a cue or sign before you go to sleep and resolve to "wake up" and be aware in the dream when you come across it. In actuality, you are sending this sign to yourself, because it is your own mind that produces your dreams.

11 Dream Signs

Dream signs are quite simply cues that you are dreaming, and are a common form of inducing lucid dreams. A dream sign can be whatever you feel guided to use, from the everyday to the extraordinary. Your dream sign will likely take the form of things or events that are considered impossible or highly improbable in the waking world. Some examples of dream signs include:

1. breathing under water
2. flying, or moving in bizarrely long jumps
3. extra-large or extra-small objects or people (think of Alice in Wonderland drinking the shrinking and growing potions)
4. unusual colors such as purple skies, blue dogs or green cats
5. disappearing or dissolving solid objects

Chapter 17

Messages from the Angels and Mermaids

The glory of God is in man fully alive.
- St. Irenaeus

The True Meaning of Baptism

The Mermaids oversee the magic and the symbolism of the water element. We usually connect christening with the water element, but baptism by water is only one part of the story.

Baptism actually occurs in four parts, according to the four elements: The first two baptisms represent the outward swing of the pendulum, or the descent (or projection) of Spirit into matter, as signified by the earth element—Adam, the first man, translates to "man of earth"—and secondly the air element, which stands for the Sons and Daughters of God (the Spirit) joining the Sons and Daughters of Man and reminding humans who have become entirely unaware and enmeshed in matter of the true origin of the human being. These two elements can be said to correspond to "the Word" (earth) and "the Breath" (air) of God (or Source).

The second pair of baptisms represents the inward swing of the pendulum, or the journey home to God—Spirit is again becoming aware of itself; in a human body. Baptism by water, which is the Christ-ening of John the Baptist, is the first of these. Incidentally, this method of baptism was foregrounded in the Piscean Age; the Age that started with Jesus Christ's birth and is now nearing its final throes. Finally, and conclusively, there is the baptism of Jesus Christ, which is that of the Holy Spirit finding its perfection, or complete expression, in man. This is the baptism of fire.

In these four elements or symbolic baptisms the story of human consciousness evolution is revealed, and the combined work of John the Baptist and of Jesus produced a synthesis on the ascension pathway—or the way back home to ourselves, and to our Source—which shows us God's plan and the goal of all human endeavors.

John the Baptist granted the baptism of water which represents purification of the emotional body; which must always be a preliminary step to the purification by fire. The baptism in the river Jordan symbolizes the purification of the principles in man, just as Christ and His baptism reveals to us the Divine in man and the purification which follows the activity of that Divine Spirit in the lower nature.

When John the Baptist uttered the words: "He shall increase but I must decrease", he spoke as a disciple, referring to his lower nature. The Divine Spirit, the Christ Consciousness in the heart, has to increase and the lower self must decrease to recognize the Divinity of the soul.

John the Baptist is called the "precursor" and "the Prophet of the Most High" who was sent (or embodied) so that "the prophecy might be fulfilled". In the very first comment that Jesus makes in the Bible about John the Baptist, he says that John is "Elias, which was for to come". The fourth Gospel tells us that, "There was a man sent from God, whose name was John".

St. John the Baptist and Jesus the Christ have come to reveal to us the Alpha and Omega of human evolution. This evolution takes place in consciousness and is like the swing of a pendulum. First, we are pure consciousness and we slowly project ourselves into form—into materiality—for the sheer creative play, joy and fun of it.

As our consciousness becomes more and more enmeshed and entangled with matter we lose awareness of our spiritual origin. When matter becomes extremely dense—as it is on Earth in the third dimension—we may think that we are only bodies with a brain who are born and then perish and die; never to rise again. This is the extreme point of the pendulum and when it swings back, we are on a journey of return; home to our True Origin and our True Self.

Of course, this true self, or divine spark, is always with us because it is our very nature and beingness; but as spirit gets entangled in matter, we may forget, or turn away, from this awareness. Water (as represented by John and his baptism) purifies and heals our emotions and our heart chakra so that the fire (as signified in the overcoming of the man Jesus who became the Christ) of the Divine Flame can blaze at our hearts—in perfect balance of Divine power, Divine love and Divine wisdom.

World Ages and 2012

Archangel Michael represents the first Ray of Divine Light, the blue ray, which brings us the Divine Will and Divine Power. Michael works with the element of fire. The Austrian mystic and educator Rudolf Steiner had a strong connection with Archangel Michael since birth, when he was baptized as a sickly infant in the Church of St. Michael. In his book *The Archangel Michael: His Mission and Ours*, he writes:

"The Michael age has dawned. Hearts begin to have thoughts. Enthusiasm no longer flows from mystical obscurity, but from the inner clarity that thought conveys. To grasp this is to receive Michael into one's soul. Thoughts that today seek to grasp the spirit must spring from hearts that beat for Michael as the fiery cosmic prince of thought." [45]

Imagine the world as it might appear to a mouse wandering on-stage during a performance of Shakespeare's "Hamlet". In front of your eyes, you witness a great drama unfold; filled with exotic colors, sounds, and complex events. Yet, because of your limited perspective, the meaning of it all eludes you. You are unable to grasp the multi-layered significance of this drama, or understand how these assorted building blocks fit into an overarching narrative that is being acted out in several acts. Only by understanding the underlying fabric that binds the separate, transitory elements together can you truly recognize the way in which they all constitute integral facets of a broader pattern of meaning, a coherent story—profound, remarkable and celebrated.

Nearly One Galactic Year (26,000 years) ago the Golden Age of the Empire of the Sun was made manifest, when humanity lived in peace, love, harmony and prosperity greater than we can envision at the moment. As our planet Earth orbits around the central sun, we are now astrologically entering the Age of Aquarius, ruled by the air element, as we leave the Age of Pisces which, ruled by the water element, lasted for the past 2100 years. We are now on the cusp, or maximum swing of the pendulum, feeling both the vibrations of a past age and the dawn of a new age.

To the Mayan people, Venus was (and is to others to this day) a very important planet, heavily tied in to their creation and "world-age" mythologies. Interestingly—and significantly, I think—Venus is the planet that is "exalted" (that is, attains its optimal expression) in Pisces. Venus is considered by the Mayans to be a central character in the transition from one world age to the next. As a result of this, the ancient Maya made it their objective to accurately track its voyage through the heavens, most precisely relative to the earth's own orbit.

The primary method employed by the Maya to keep track of Venus was by noting the successive passage of conjunctions between Venus and the Earth. The Maya invented, or initiated, the 260 day cycle to track the occurrence of successive conjunctions involving the Earth and Venus over a full 2000 year grand cycle.

The Pleiades are a group of seven stars who are visible as twinkling lights in a clear night sky and who are sometimes referred to as the Seven Sisters. The Aztecs, who derived their astronomical knowledge from the Maya, called them the *Cabrillas*.

According to accounts produced by the early Spanish explorers in the 16th century, the ceremony which was held to mark the end of a sheaf period every 52 years was precisely synchronized with the observation of the Pleiades star group at midnight, on the one particular night of the year when it appeared exactly upon the meridian.

The Mayans were also responsible for developing and establishing a calendar of far greater span and duration; one that was based upon a recurring time period of precisely 1,872,000 days, equal to 5,125.36 years. The name given to this calendar is the Long Count. Solar days were counted in numbers which corresponded to a particular name depending on the time period they covered. In total there are five major time cycles that comprise the calendar, each fractionally harmonious with the full measure of the primary interval (1,872,000 days). 1 Solar Day is named a *Kin*, 20 Solar Days are a *Unial*, 360 Solar Days are a *Tun*, 7,200 Solar Days are a *Katun* and 144,000 Solar Days are a *Baktun*.

The end of the astronomical Long Count Mayan calendar on 21st December 2012 is seen by many as the astronomical and energetic shift to the Age of Aquarius which is accompanied by a simultaneous shift in consciousness towards ascension. Humankind is again awakening to the divine spark or the divine essence within.

The Piscean Age is the 2100 year cycle that follows the Age of Aries. Around the year 2100 B.C. we entered the age of Aries and 2100 years ago we entered the age of Pisces. Pisces is the age of Universal Peace and is sponsored (or overseen) by Jesus the Christ. The Aquarian Age is the 2100 year cycle that follows the Piscean Age and is sponsored by the Ascended Master Saint Germain and his divine complement, the Ascended Lady Master Portia.

Those who have assumed the feminine polarity after the ascension are called Ascended Lady Masters. Divine complement is another term used for the Twin Flame, the soul's masculine or feminine counterpart. You only have one twin flame. These two souls (soul complements or soul halves) share a unique blueprint. The Aquarian Age is the age of Freedom.

Among the manifestations of the Piscean Age was the spread of a global religion which made extensive use of water symbols: baptism by water, holy water, healing springs (such as Lourdes), walking on water, changing water into wine. Indeed, while researching astrology and symbolism, I discovered that Christianity affords many associations to the water sign of Pisces.

Within us all is the potential to "ascend", which means to attain a higher state of consciousness. As we are all divine sparks, made in the likeness of the Creator, created out of the only Substance available—Itself, we all have one destiny: to ascend and to return to Source.

On this journey back home, we have a lot of help—the Angels, the Ascended Masters, the Mermaids, Dolphins, Fairies and other Elementals are all here to help and assist us to fulfill our purpose.

Most importantly of all, though, you have yourself. All that you seek lies within you.

Rumi, the 13th century mystic, expresses this great truth and summarizes the Divine Alchemy of the soul's journey of transformation from "dust into pure gold", or from matter back to Spirit that reveals the eternal knowledge that *you are never alone.* [46]

Your Source is made manifest in the Divine Spark within your Heart.

You lack a foot to travel?
Then journey into yourself
And like a mine of rubies
receive the sunbeams print
Out of yourself such a journey
will lead you to your self,
It leads to transformation
of dust into pure gold!

Endnotes

1. Rudolf Steiner, *Theosophy -- An Introduction to the Supersensible Knowledge of the World and the Destination of Man* (New York, NY: Anthroposophic Press, 1971), pp. 102-103.

2. Juan Ruiz Minchero, *The Voice from the Jordan*, (Victoria, B.C.: Trafford Publishing), p. 108.

3. Kevin J. Todeschi, editor, *Edgar Cayce on the Akashic Records* (Virginia Beach, VA: A.R.E. Press), p. 6.

4. Damigeron, translated by Patricia Tahil, edited by Joel Radcliffe, *The Virtues of Stones* (Seattle, WA: Ars Obscura, 1989)

5. Pliny (the Elder), translated by John Bostock and H. T. Riley, *The Natural History, Volume 6* (London: Henry Bohn, 1857), p. 414.

6. Rainer Maria Rilke, *Letters to Merline, 1919-1922* (St. Paul, MN: Paragon House, 1988)

7. Kevin J. Todeschi, editor, *Edgar Cayce on the Akashic Records* (Virginia Beach, VA: A.R.E. Press), p. 47.

8. Mary Jane Ryan, *A Grateful Heart: Daily Blessings for the Evening Meal from Buddha to the "Beatles"* (York Beach, ME: Red Wheel/ Weiser, 1994), p. 44.

9. Rudolf Steiner, *Theosophy*, p. 105.

10. Elena Ivanovna Roerich, *Letters to America*, in 4 Volumes (1923-1952), Vol. 4 (Moscow: Sfera, 1999)

11. Mark L. Prophet, Elizabeth Clare Prophet, *The Science of the Spoken Word* (Gardiner, MT: Summit University Press, 1965), p. 114.

12. Elizabeth Clare Prophet, *Saint Germain: Master Alchemist* (Gardiner, MT: Summit University Press, 2004)

13. Edgar Cayce, *Edgar Cayce's Story of Jesus*, selected and edited by Jeffrey Furst (New York, NY: Berkley/ The Penguin Group, 1968), p. 43.

14. John Sutton, Ph.D., "The Tuaoi Stone: An Enigma", *A.R.E. Journal* (January 1974)

15. Edgar Cayce, *The Psychic Sense: How to Awaken Your Sixth Sense to Solve Life's Problems and Seize Opportunities* (Virginia Beach, VA: A.R.E. Press, 2006 [1971]), p. 120.

16. Simone Gabbay, *Nourishing the Body Temple* (Virginia Beach, VA: A.R.E. Press, 1999), p. 102.

17. Ernst Haeckel, *History of Creation*, translated by E. Ray Lankester and Kegan Paul, 3rd edition, Vol. I. (London: Trench & Co., 1883), pp. 360-62.

18. Matt. 12:37.

19. Elizabeth Clare Prophet, *Saint Germain: Master Alchemist*, p. 86.

20. For more information, see <http://www.timesonline.co.uk/tol/news/science/article6973994.ece>

21. For more information on the major Greek/Latin gods and goddesses and their histories, consult <http://www.unrv.com/culture/major-roman-god-list.php>

22. Charles Avery, *A School of Dolphins* (London: Thames & Hudson, 2009), p. 91.

23. Phylarchus, cited in Athenaeus, *The Deipnosophists*, translated by C. D. Yonge, Book 13 (London: Henry G. Bohn, 1854), pp. 601-612.

24. Athenaeus, *The Deipnosophists*, translated by C. D. Yonge, Book 13 (London: Henry G. Bohn, 1854), pp. 601-612.

25. Kahlil Gibran, *The Prophet* (Teddington, Middlesex: Echo Library, 2006), p. 6.

26. Ralph Waldo Emerson, *Journals of Ralph Waldo Emerson, with Annotations - 1824-1832*, edited by Edward Waldo Emerson and Waldo Emerson Forbes (London: Constable, 1910), p. 395.

27. John Randolph Price, *The Abundance Book* (Carlsbad, CA: Hay House, 2005)

28. See <http://www.universal-tao.com/dark_room/nutrition.html>

29. See < http://www.springboard4health.com/notebook/proteins_tryptophan.html> for a full listing of tryptophan- rich foods.

30. For further scientific studies and research, see <http://www.algamar.com/valor.php?id=2>

31. Hassan Amjad, M.D., *Elixir of Life: Meditations over a Cup of Tea* (Raleigh, NC: Lulu/Amjad, 2007), p. 80.

32. David Servan-Schreiber, *Anticancer: A New Way of Life* (London: Michael Joseph/ Penguin, 2008)

33. See <http://www.teapalace.co.uk/Gyokuro-Asahi-P303 >, or similar sites, to order online.

34. I Corinthians 12:8-11.

35. I Corinthians 15:37-41.

36. Rom. 5:5.

37. Elizabeth Clare Prophet, *Saint Germain: Master Alchemist*, p. 87.

38. Matt. 6:6.

39. Antoine de Saint-Exupery, *Wind, Sand, and Stars* (London: Penguin Classics, 2000 [1939])

40. Plato, *Timaeus*, chapters 22-23; cited in Gregory Vlastos, *Plato's Universe* (Las Vegas, NV: Parmenides/The University of Chicago Press, 2006), pp. 66-82.

41. C.G. Jung, *On the Nature of the Psyche*, translated by R.F.C. Hull (Princeton, NJ: Princeton University Press, 1969), p.95.

42. Mark Thurston, *Dreams: Tonight's Answers for Tomorrow's Questions (An Edgar Cayce Guide)* (New York, NY: St. Martin's Press, 1996)

43. Frederik van Eeden, "A Study of Dreams" in *Proceedings of the Society for Psychical Research* (1913), p. 26.

Gabbay, Simone, *Nourishing the Body Temple* (Virginia Beach, VA: A.R.E. Press, 1999)

Gibran, Kahlil, *The Garden of the Prophet, Lazarus and His Beloved, Sand and Foam* (Teddington, Middlesex: Echo Library, 2009)

Gibran, Kahlil, *The Prophet* (Teddington, Middlesex: Echo Library, 2006)

Haeckel, Ernst, *History of Creation*, translated by E. Ray Lankester and Kegan Paul, 3rd edition, Vol. I. (London: Trench & Co., 1883)

Jung, C.G., *On the Nature of the Psyche*, translated by R.F.C. Hull (Princeton, NJ: Princeton University Press, 1969)

Minchero, Juan Ruiz, *The Voice from the Jordan*, (Victoria, B.C.: Trafford Publishing)

Phylarchus, cited in Athenaeus, *The Deipnosophists*, translated by C. D. Yonge, Book 13 (London: Henry G. Bohn, 1854)

Plato, *Timaeus*, chapters 22-23, cited in Gregory Vlastos, *Plato's Universe* (Las Vegas, NV: Parmenides/The University of Chicago Press, 2006)

Pliny (the Elder), translated by John Bostock and H. T. Riley, *The Natural History, Volume 6* (London: Henry Bohn, 1857)

Price, John Randolph, *The Abundance Book* (Carlsbad, CA: Hay House, 2005)

Prophet, Elizabeth Clare, *Saint Germain: Master Alchemist* (Gardiner, MT: Summit University Press, 2004)

Prophet, Mark L., Prophet, Elizabeth Clare, *The Science of the Spoken Word* (Gardiner, MT: Summit University Press, 1965)

Rilke, Rainer Maria, *Letters to Merline, 1919-1922* (St. Paul, MN: Paragon House, 1988)

Roerich, Elena Ivanovna, *Letters to America*, in 4 Volumes (1923-1952), Vol. 4 (Moscow: Sfera, 1999)

Rumi, Jalal al-Din, edited by William C. Chittick, *The Sufi Path of Love: The Spiritual Teachings of Rumi* (Albany, NY: State University of New York Press, 1984)

Ryan, Mary Jane, *A Grateful Heart: Daily Blessings for the Evening Meal from Buddha to the "Beatles"* (York Beach, ME: Red Wheel/ Weiser, 1994)

Saint-Exupery, Antoine de, *Wind, Sand, and Stars* (London: Penguin Classics, 2000 [1939])

Servan-Schreiber, David, *Anticancer: A New Way of Life* (London: Michael Joseph/ Penguin, 2008)

Steiner, Rudolf, *The Archangel Michael: His Mission and Ours*, edited and introduced by Christopher Bamford (Herndon, VA: SteinerBooks, 1994)

Steiner, Rudolf, *Theosophy—An Introduction to the Supersensible Knowledge of the World and the Destination of Man* (New York, NY: Anthroposophic Press, 1971)

Sutton, John, "The Tuaoi Stone: An Enigma", *A.R.E. Journal* (January 1974)

Thurston, Mark, *Dreams: Tonight's Answers for Tomorrow's Questions (An Edgar Cayce Guide)* (New York, NY: St. Martin's Press, 1996)

Todeschi, Kevin J., editor, *Edgar Cayce on the Akashic Records* (Virginia Beach, VA: A.R.E. Press)